WINGS OVER EASTERN ENGLAND

Revised by Minimax Books in 1992

Original Text

by

G M Dixon

and

J Rippon

Many of the photographs used in this book have been provided by John Dunnell of North Walsham, Mrs McIntyre of Heacham, The Imperial War Museum and the Ministry of Defence

ISBN 0 906791 74 X

WINGS OVER EASTERN ENGLAND

Contents

Chapter 1. TAKE OFF

The one-hundred miles (160 kms) or so of water which separate our island from the European mainland have proved both friend and foe to our fighting forces. Eastern England was one of the obvious choices for Royal Air Force bases and is certainly one of the acknowledged homes of the R.A.F. The story of either would be incomplete without the inclusion of the other.

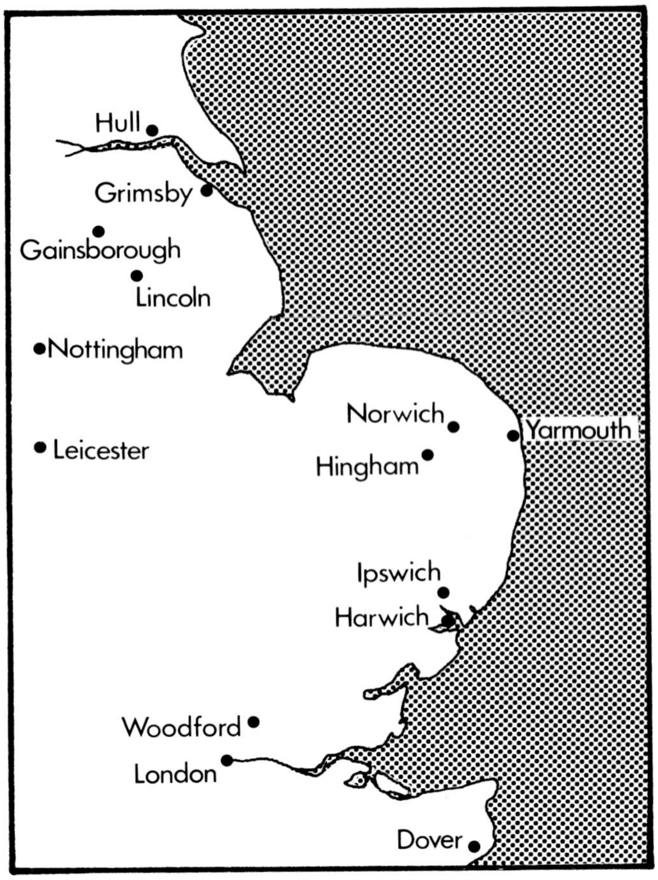

Map of Eastern England and North Sea showing areas of interest

Ever since aircraft were invented, "magnificent men in their flying machines" have been drawn to the area, for the lie of the land favours the aeronaut; its firm, flat fenlands are perfect for take-offs and landings and the whole area is sparsely populated.

In the early years of this century, both civil and military bodies became excited at the prospect of flight. For the civilian it meant an interest and a craze that led to the fame of a few and the death of many. Balloons, airships and powered craft vied with each other to prove their superiority, and the fortunes of each were influenced by the bravado, skill and enterprise of its developers.

The Royal Naval Air Service and the Army's Flying Corps saw the fighting potential in aircraft and soon airfields took shape on the flat grasslands outside the garrison towns of Eastern England. The first base was opened at Orfordness in 1912 and quickly followed by bases at Skegness, Thetford and Felixstowe.

Aircraft 8422, an RE8 (known colloquially as a 'Harry Tate'). This type first flew in mid-1916

Remains of a crashed Zeppelin

The First World War

A number of World War I airfields built to defend our coastal regions began as humble grass fields with the hardy airmen living in tents around the perimeter. In 1915 Narborough Naval base was opened near Marham in Norfolk. Intended to be a defence against Zeppelin attacks, it was later taken over by the Royal Flying Corps as a fighter training base and remained so until the end of the war. Fowlmere played a similar role and Duxford, built in 1919, was to become one of the most famous airfields of World War II. Felixstowe was another Naval base, opened before 1914 it served as a flying boat station, experimental station, training unit and, following serious damage to the slipways in the 1953 East Coast floods, flew helicopters from 1956-1961. This base finally closed in 1962 and is now incorporated into Felixstowe docks.

Aeroplanes were used by the Navy for coastal patrol, but primarily the stations in Eastern England were built so that pilots could be trained for reconnaissance duties in France, their aircraft replacing the vulnerable balloons. In these stations young men were given minimum flying instruction before being sent to France to face the superior craft of the German Air Force. Many young men felt compelled to join either the R.F.C. or the R.N.A.S. after watching the aircraft in the skies and listening to the tales of returned heroes.

It was only a decade before that the American Samuel Franklin Cody had completed the first powered flight in this country and aeroplanes were still frail crafts of wood, canvas and wire with an engine affixed.

Flying could only occur when weather conditions were ideal, a wind of 10 knots or more making handling almost impossible. Low cloud and rain added hazards as no navigation equipment was fitted. Also, as the cockpit was open, both pilot and engine were affected by prevailing weather conditions. Forced landings were frequent due to the general low flying level and these often resulted in death. As design and engines improved larger planes were built which were able to carry two people, one to pilot and one to observe. Using maps and charts the observer would follow landmarks, marking enemy troop positions and supply routes. He also had to watch out for enemy aircraft and if these were met they would fight with grappling irons, grenades, revolvers and darts, but only rarely were these methods successful. Soon observers had automatic guns fitted on pivots so that they could shoot at enemy aircraft. Unfortunately, the wings of the biplane restricted vision and firing; the propellor and the wire between the wings prevented any forward firing, the tail fin and rudder precluded any shooting to the rear, and if the enemy was underneath the gun could not be lowered enough to bring it to bear, and so the method taught was to manoeuvre slightly below and to the side of the target.

First aircraft to crash at Cranwell, in 1916. It was a Handley-Page 0/400, The R.F.C.'s standard heavy bomber

In 1915 the Dutch aircraft engineer Anthony Fokker built a war plane and offered the design to the British Government who, strangely enough, rejected it. The Germans accepted his offer and built the plane. Shortly afterwards his engineers designed a gun with an interrupter mechanism that enabled the aeroplane to be used as a gun platform, the pilot, sighting the target through a fixed gunsight, moved the whole aeroplane to bring his guns to bear. Thus head on attacks were possible and British losses were heavy.

Fokker E.111 Aircraft, showing interrupter mechanism

The Fokker aeroplane was also unusual in that it had only one wing mounted below the cockpit. This improved visibility considerably, made the craft lighter and faster; factors which the Germans used to great advantage.

However, the British made great progress with their aircraft design and were soon able to fight on more equal terms with the Germans. New tactics were continually being employed to try and engage and outwit the enemy and gone were the days when lone observation aircraft used carrier pigeons to take messages back to base in the event of an emergency.

As more and more aircraft were deployed some uniform training programmes had to be started and quite naturally these were founded near large Army or Navy training bases. This proved unsatisfactory and the R.N.A.S. decided in 1915 to centralise training for aircrew at Cranwell, Lincolnshire. It was an enormous camp by any standards and covered 3,000 acres (1200 hectares), so large in fact that a single track railway was built to service it from the main line at Sleaford, and today the railway station is still in use as the main guard room on the camp.

Old Station/Todays Guardroom at Cranwell

Because airships had a far greater carrying capacity than aeroplanes, concentrated efforts were made to develop the airship further. An airship station was opened at Pulham Market in 1916 and it was from here that the R33 and R34 flew, the latter being famous for being the first to make the double Atlantic crossing. It is interesting to note that Nevil Shute was the Chief Stress Engineer in the airship test centre at Cambridge and his story may be read in his book "Slide Rule". Barnes Wallis, of bouncing bomb fame, worked with Shute on the design of the R.100, sister ship of the fated R.101 which subsequently crashed and ended the era of the airship.

R33 Airship over Pulham Market

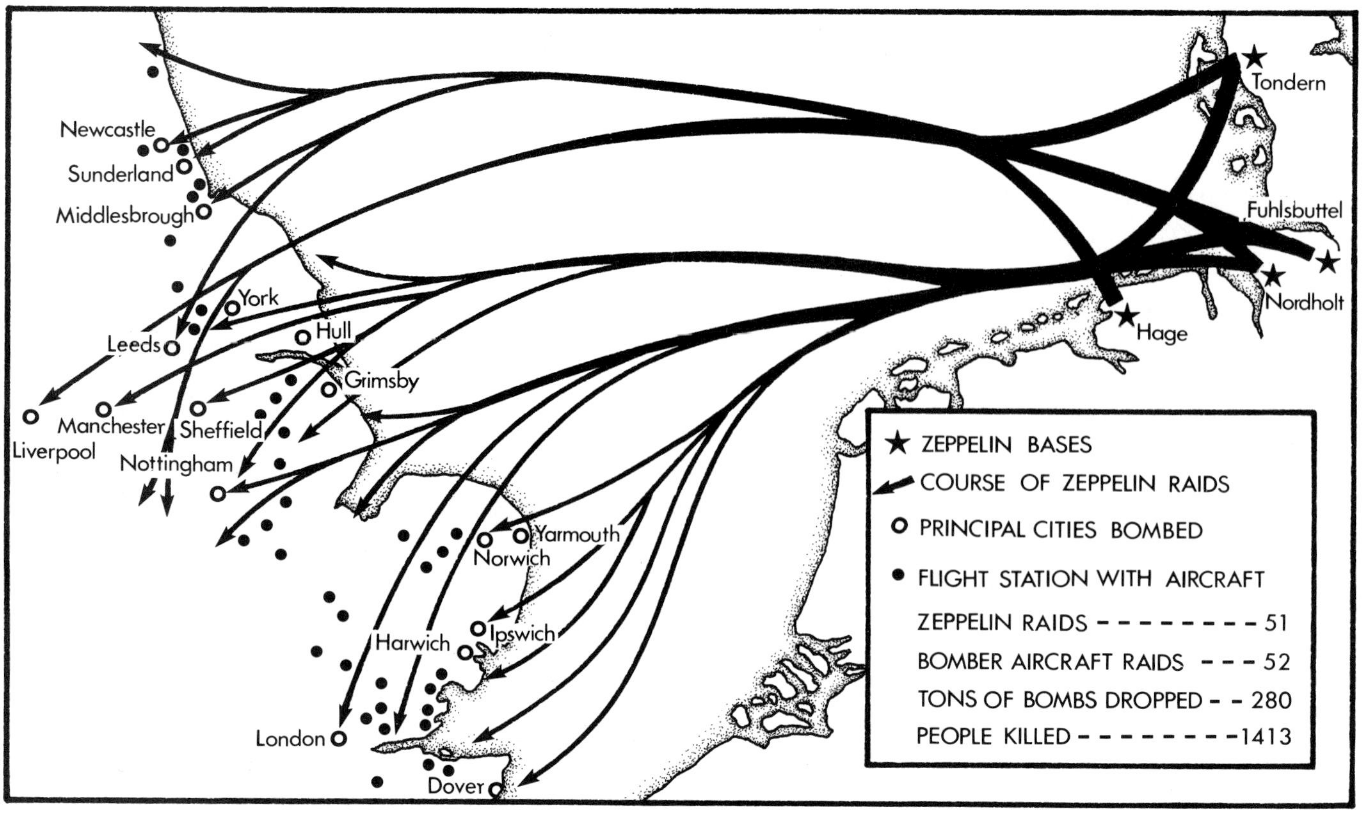

The first Zeppelin airship raid on London in September, 1915, killed 13 people and injured 87, making it clear that some form of air defence was necessary. Most Royal Flying Corps forces were in France, but the Home Defence Network was quickly organised by using squadrons of fighters such as BE2's and Avro 5045's which were not considered suitable for front line service. Headquarters were established in military towns of East Anglia, each town having three airfields each with a flight of aircraft and full services including searchlights, anti-aircraft guns, transport, etc. Emergency landing fields were organised for aircraft in trouble with mechanical problems and sudden changes of weather. This Home Defence Network covered the coast from Humber to London, the Wash forming the strategic area with the station at Bircham Newton in Norfolk as Coastal Command.

Eastern England took the brunt of Zeppelin attack but airships had proved too costly to build and too vulnerable to attack. However, the rattling roar of the Zeppelin was feared as much as the whine of the V1 in a later war.

During the war many local firms assisted in the war effort. Boulton and Paul in Norwich started building aircraft in 1915 and used Mousehold Heath as their testing ground. Savages in Kings Lynn, better known for their fairground association, also produced aeroplanes which were bought by the R.F.C.

An aerial view of Cranwell main camp in 1916

Handley-Page V/1500 four engined bomber – destined never to see active service

An exciting development took place when Lt. Col. R. H. Mulock was appointed to Bircham Newton station in 1916 to form 27 Group, later 166 Squadron, the first bomber squadron. His task was to prepare for the first long range bombing attacks on Berlin. It was intended that they should be equipped with Handley-Page V/1500 four-engined bombers, but by Armistice Day only three had arrived and no raids were carried out. But, more momentously, from this anti-climax was born the idea of Bomber Command.

Lord Trenchard, the "Father of the Royal Air Force"

On 1st April, 1918, the Royal Flying Corps and the Royal Naval Air Service were amalgamated to form the Royal Air Force, much against the wishes of the respective Admirals and Generals. Lord Trenchard, following a distinguished career in the R.F.C., and despite previous disagreements with the government, was appointed Chief of Staff in 1918 to form the Royal Air Force. It was largely due to his vision of the R.A.F. as a separate force, with its own training establishment at Cranwell, and his strength of mind, that the R.A.F. developed as it did.

Lord Trenchard

Lord Trenchard also arranged for a technical training school to be established at Halton on February 5th, 1920. Until Halton was ready the young technicians trained at Cranwell and in the first intake was Frank Whittle who later invented the jet engine which effected a huge change in aircraft design. To encourage cadets to develop a mechanical aptitude each was issued with a motor cycle, which he was expected to maintain, and free petrol and oil. This came to an end after a newspaper adjudged it a 'wasteful expenditure'. The R.A.F. was happy with this for more cadets were said to be injured riding motor cycles than flying!

In the years to follow the ranks of our flying service were to be all the richer in leadership, technical expertise and many other aspects, thanks to the foresight shown by Lord Trenchard and fellow officers who spawned and nursed our Royal Air Force through its adolescence to produce the superbly trained fighting force that carried us through the early years of World War II.

Between the Wars

When the First World War ended, Britain was left with a massive air force of up-to-date warplanes, with aircraft in production and design of an advanced standard. Germany was left with no air force at all!

Nationally, the years between 1918 and 1935 were tremendously exciting for all those concerned with flying. For these were the days of record-seeking and record-breaking. Fliers thrilled the world as they set out to prove the capabilities of the aeroplane. Alcock and Brown flew across the Atlantic Ocean in 1919 and in 1927 American Charles Lindbergh made the first solo crossing of the Atlantic. In 1930 Amy Johnson was the first woman to fly solo from England to Australia.

The Schneider Trophy race for sea-planes was won in 1925 and 1926 by foreign planes, but in 1927 by Britain. This victory was achieved by a combination of aircraft designer R. J. Mitchell and the Rolls Royce engine, the duo that in later years produced the Supermarine Spitfire. Later still, in 1936, the Mildenhall to Melbourne Race was won by C. W. A. Scott and Campbell Black in the fantastic de Havilland Comet. Due to worldwide interest in flight, designers and manufacturers competing for honours and rewards, had forged great steps in the mastery of aeronautics. Bearing in mind that these machines had been designed and built by private companies with private money it was quite an achievement.

Fairey 3F pranged, 1930

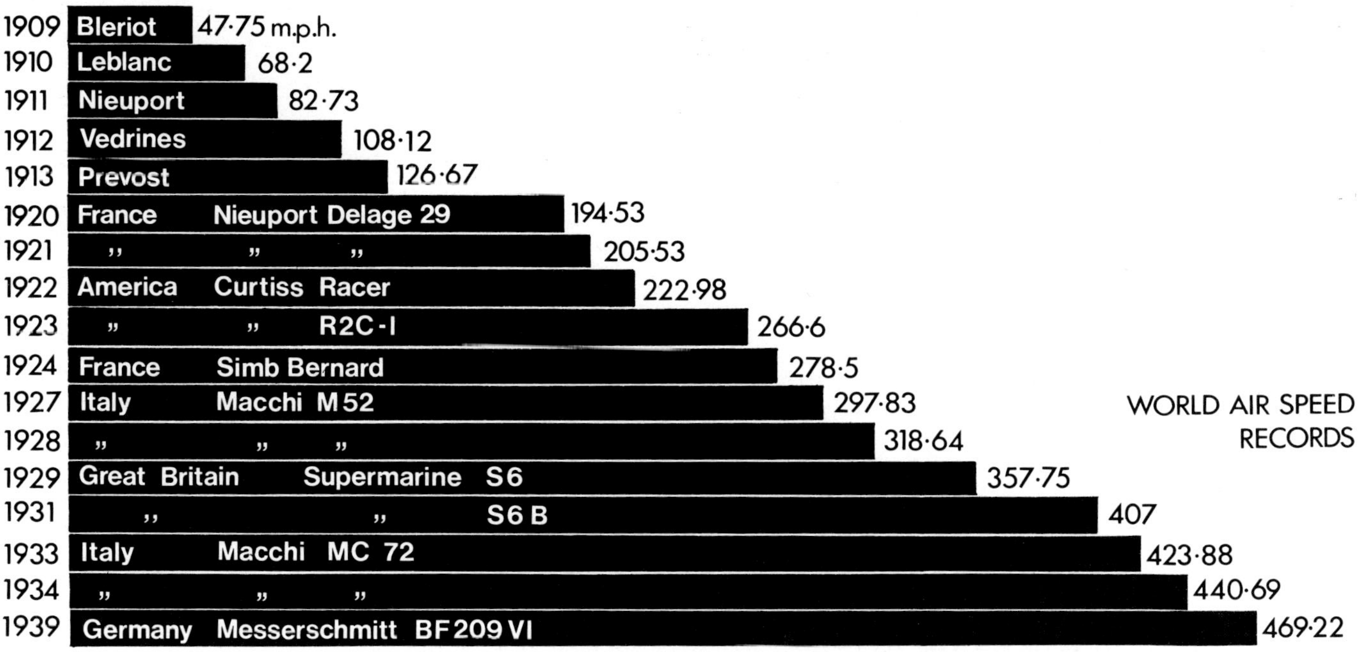

It wasn't until the middle thirties when Germany decided to re-arm that any kind of effort was made by the British government to do the same. By this time, the aeroplane had progressed way beyond the canvas-and-string stage. Most modern aircraft were of the monoplane design and built entirely of metal, fitted with radios, navigation equipment and covered cockpits.

Britain should have been ready for the onslaught of the Second World War.

Aircraft and pilot being welcomed home, Cranwell, after long distance race

PLACES TO VISIT:

The Shuttleworth Collection
Old Warden Aerodrome
Nr Biggleswade, Bedfordshire
Telephone: 076727 288

They say "Time flies at Old Warden" and, if you would like to see the Shuttleworth Collection of historic aircraft, the aerodrome is open all year round. From November through to April aeroplanes being overhauled and restored can be seen. Throughout the rest of the year various events take place, including the magnificent flying displays.

Chapter 2. AT BAY.

Expansion

When it was decided to expand the Royal Air Force in 1934 to meet the threat of the re-arming Germany, few operational bases were left in the Eastern area; Felixstowe, the seaplane base, Bircham Newton, and Duxford being the most modern. Pulham Market, the airship base was still open, but, especially after the dreadful R101 accident in France, interest in dirigibles was waning and the huge airship hangars from Pulham were moved to Cardington. In these hangars thousands of new recruits were later to be kitted out and have their first military haircuts. Another important airfield was the Aeroplane and Armament Experimental Station at Martlesham Heath where development trials were carried out.

Soon letters began popping through letterboxes of farmers and landowners in our region, notifying them to expect parties of government officials to evaluate suitable sites for military uses. Such was the pace of development that the surveyors often arrived before the letters and farm labourers told tales in the local public houses of landowners brandishing shotguns to warn off the intruders. But the shock of seeing the surveyors was soon belittled by the sight of bulldozers levelling hedges, lorries bringing in building materials, and the formation of workparties, constructing airfields in fields which contained half grown crops. At first the airfields had grass runways which were adequate for light bombers and fighters, but with the new heavy bombers being developed, many expansion airfields would have to be closed later for concrete runways to be laid.

With the invasion of Austria by Germany in March 1938, the British government were left with no alternative but to prepare for all out war. The Air Ministry was given permission to order twelve thousand aircraft for delivery by early 1940. When war was declared on 3rd September 1939, the front line strength of the Royal Air Force was 1911 aircraft of both bombers and fighters.

Aerial view of Bircham Newton base in 1930

The common features of a typical war-time airfield are shown in the diagram below.

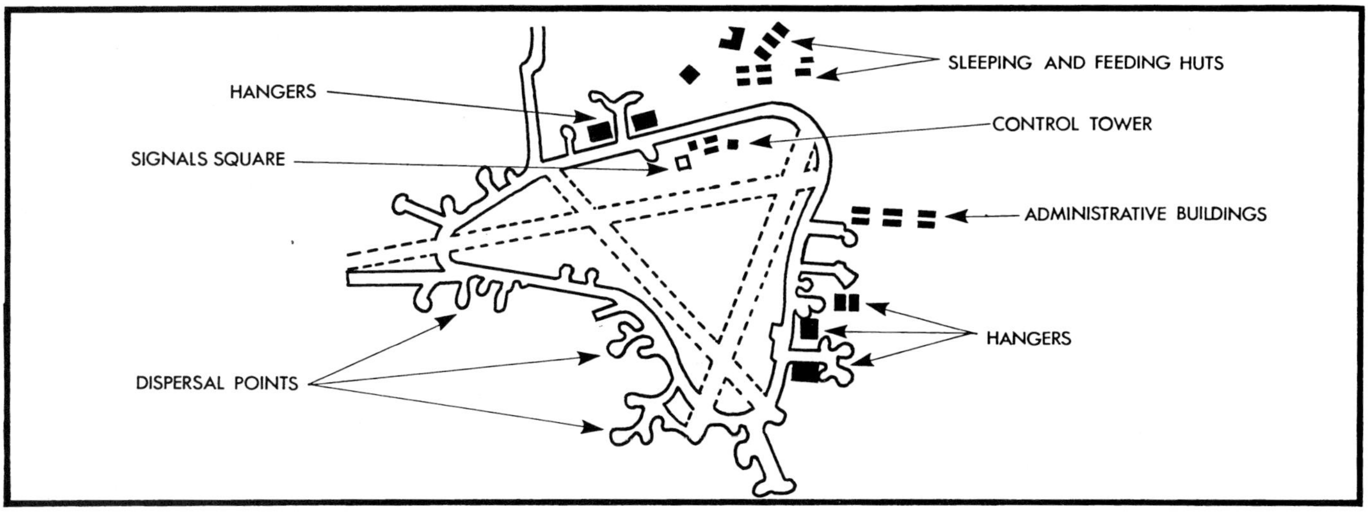

The R.A.F. training establishment at Cranwell was revitalised to meet the new demand for a great number of pilots and flying crew. Training at Digby and Duxford was also expanded to meet the growing threat from Germany.

War Time Airfields

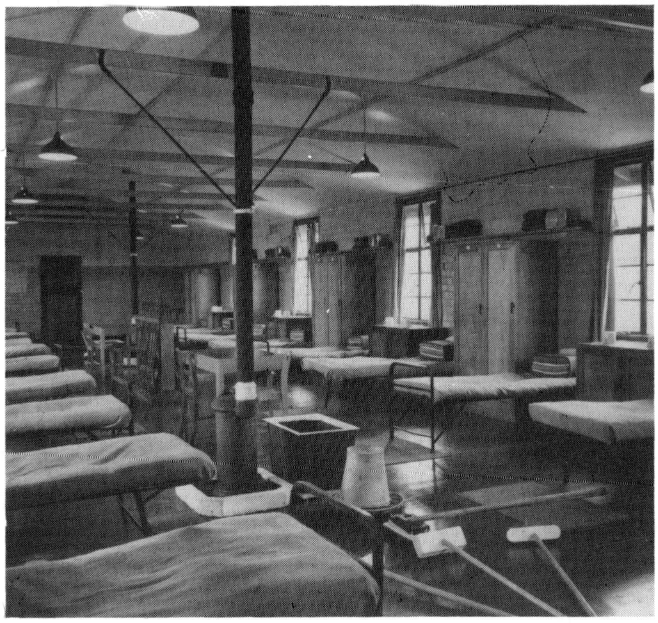

Typical billet

In spite of the 1934 expansion there were less than twenty five airfields in Eastern England at the outbreak of war. This was obviously inadequate and in a flurry of activity, many new airfields were built. Coltishall was the first of the wartime airfields to open in June 1940, and Waterbeach was the first one with a concrete runway to be opened in 1941. Until concrete runways were provided, the "hard" surface was either grass or a cinder covered strip. The main runways lay in the direction of the prevailing wind and the new concrete runways enabled the use of Drem lighting which was an invaluable night flying aid. As most of East Anglia was without electricity the airfields had to build temporary generating units.

Housing also was a very hurried affair. Initially tents were used for the men and camouflage nets for the aircraft. Due to the time taken to remove the nets in case of attack, and the vulnerability of hangars, aeroplanes were often sheltered under a belt of trees. However, hangars were needed for maintenance and the initial blister type hangars were later superseded in the 1942 period by prefabricated rectangular metal hangars made by The Tees-side Engineering Company.

Such services as adequate roads, water and sewage facilities were seen as a priority but first, and by a long way, was the essential purpose of keeping the enemy at bay.

In 1939-40 these Hawker Harts were temporarily housed in canvas hangars which were ravaged by gale force winds

DEFENDING THE MIDLANDS AND EASTERN ENGLAND

Fighters

The fighter bases were established in Eastern England so that the manufacturing cities in the Midlands could be defended. In the expanding tactics of war, the possibility of the enemy flying over to bomb and wreck the nucleus of the war effort was recognised, and the necessity for defence fighters was apparent. It was planned to establish squadrons of fighters to ward off attacks and, in the 1940's when the Luftwaffe pounded the cities and towns of Britain, the value of this was seen. Defiants, made by Boulton and Paul of Norwich, Hurricanes and Spitfires were the aircraft most commonly used.

Boulton and Paul Defiant, a highly successful night fighter, from No 264 Squadron based at Kirton-in-Lindsay

One of the 'Boys in Blue'

Self-Help

To help meet the huge cost of funding the construction of bombers and fighters, the civilian population was encouraged to collect scrap materials of all kinds and to organise fund-raising events to purchase equipment. The Government sought the help of Lord Beaverbrook, the newspaper tycoon, in this respect, and he co-ordinated the "War Effort". Targets were publicised:-

Spitfire	£6,000
Hurricane	£4,500
Wellington	£25,000
Pair of binoculars	£17
Depth charge	£25

In the log book of Stoke Holy Cross School near Norwich the entry for 24th April, 1941, reads: "The children gave a little entertainment today after school and 30/- (£1.50) was raised for the Spitfire fund. The amount will be sent to Lord Beaverbrook."

Raids on Norwich

Lord Beaverbrook's son, Wing Commander Max Aitken, was in charge of 68 Squadron based at Coltishall. Just before midnight on April 27th, 1941, German bombers flew in over Wells-on-Sea to make a night raid on Norwich. Local bases, including Coltishall, were put on alert, but no contact with the enemy bombers was made and three people were killed and two hundred injured. Two days later Norwich was again raided without loss to the enemy, and with their confidence mounting they returned the following evening. This time our night-fighters destroyed three enemy aircraft. About a week later the Germans returned, but this time they were beaten off and one raider was even brought down by a barrage balloon at Stoke Holy Cross. There was great consternation next morning when only three of the crew of four were found; the fourth was never traced, despite searches and reported sightings.

Later in 1943 the Germans resumed their air attacks on Britain, and dropped many different types of bombs, including the dreaded butterfly bomb. On one occasion a lone German raider was chased out to sea, tracked by RADAR at Neatishead, and eventually caught and shot down into the north sea, by Flying Officer Boyle.

The W.A.A.F., Women's Auxiliary Air Force, was formed in July 1939. These women were used predominantly for clerical and communications work

Enter the Italians

The Italians made a few half-hearted attempts to attack Harwich by air, one on November 11th, 1940. No. 257 Squadron from Martlesham Heath, among others, scrambled, and so frightened and decimated the Italians that they never returned!

To the memory of the undermentioned members of 753rd Squadron 458th Bomber Group 2nd Bombardment Division U.S.A.A.F. who died near this spot 24th November, 1944.

The pilot of the bomber as his last act avoided crashing on this and surrounding cottages thus preventing the possible loss of civilian lives.

Second Lieutenant J. Dooley, Philadelphia, P.A.
Second Lieutenant Arthur Akin Junior, Portsmouth V.A.
Second Lieutenant Paul E. Gorman, Brooklyn
Staff Sergeant John H. Jones, Texas
Staff Sergeant Paul A. Wadsworth, Texas
Staff Sergeant Oscar B. Nelson, Washington
Staff Sergeant John A. Philips, New York
Staff Sergeant John P. Quirk, Indiannapolis
Staff Sergeant Ralph Von Bergen, Denver, Colorado

The Words of a Commemorative plaque in Norwich

Mix Up

Although aircrew were trained in the matter of aircraft identification, mistakes were sometimes made by pilots at night. On one occasion, during a raid on Norwich, two Westland Whirlwinds flying from Matlaske saw what they thought was a Junkers 88. They attacked it, and in the ensuing mêlée one Whirlwind returned to Matlaske, the other was shot down, and the 'Junkers 88', turning out to be a British Blenheim, flew off.

Battle of Britain

The aircrews of Eastern England featured significantly in the Battle of Britain. Indeed the first German plane to be shot down in the battle fell to Sergeant Robertson of 66 Squadron flying from Coltishall.

Wing Commander Douglas Bader, later to become a legend, leading the 242 Squadron of Hurricanes from Coltishall, also took part in the Battle of Britain. 15th September, 1940, was a great day for him when he destroyed two German bombers out of the nineteen shot down that day, and winning thereby the D.S.O. The exploits of this brave airman who lost both legs in a flying accident early in his career only to overcome his handicap and become one of our fighter aces needs no retelling. Bader was involved in the formation of what became known as the "Big Wing" or the "Duxford Wing", which figured prominently in many large air battles.

Douglas Bader

Hurricane about to take off

Home

Typical of the stations was Castle Camps in Cambridgeshire where No. 73 Squadron had just arrived at the end of August 1940. Immediately hurled into action, mainly in the defence of London, they flew from a field where they slept in tents, ate in a marquee in the woods, took off from a grass strip and parked their planes on the grass. Flying up to ten sorties every day they fought German fighters and bombers of all kinds. After a morning take-off on September 15th, 1940, they sallied forth again in the afternoon with the remaining six serviceable Hurricanes to meet one hundred enemy bombers over Kent. They managed to shoot down three before returning to base.

The Big Wing

Faced with the huge onslaught on London of hundreds of German bombers, the idea of the Big Wing was born. So that the force of fighters could be co-ordinated many squadrons of fighters from Eastern England assembled over Duxford, before diving off to London and the South East.

Fighters, left behind in the East, had the task of wiping out the German planes that had escaped from London and sought a quieter route back to Germany.

After the Battle of Britain died down in November, 1940, there were continual raids on the towns and cities of the Midlands and Eastern counties until early 1941, then there was a respite until early the following year. The population of these areas were to suffer many heavy blitzes as the Germans continued to pound them until 1943 when the raids slackened off a great deal.

Five Supermarine Spitfire Mk1 fighters flying in echelon starboard formation

All this time the R.A.F. kept up a continual guard, harrying and destroying the German planes in a routine but heroic way.

Escort Missions

In addition to defending the towns and cities, the fighters were also used to defend shipping, bombers and troop movements. Using their extreme manoeuvrability and facilities the fighters could be adapted and armed to deal with all kinds of attack.

Escorted shipping

Escorting the bombers

When some Blenheims of 226 Squadron from Ipswich were given the task of bombing two power stations near Cologne in daylight on 12th August, 1941, three Spitfire squadrons from Duxford and Coltishall were detailed to escort the bombers home. After an eventful and successful raid, the bombers met the Spitfires just over the Dutch coast. Immediately the East Anglian squadrons were flung into action by Messerschmitts which were chasing the bombers. The Spitfires seemed to revel in the battle as they fearlessly dived on the German fighters and drove them off leaving some Messerschmitts in the sea, the tired Blenheims being left free to fly home.

Danger of Rendezvous

When twelve Venturas from Methwold in Norfolk were ordered to bomb the steelworks at Ijmuiden in Holland on May 3rd, 1943, it was to be a disastrous mission.

Due to rendezvous with escort fighters over Flushing the fighters were early, alerted the enemy and the usual dog fights took place. With fuel running low the fighters had to break off and head for home before the bombers arrived. The Luftwaffe were waiting for the unescorted bombers and with the exception of one who, though badly damaged, made it home, the remainder were all shot down.

After his release from a German P.O.W. camp at the end of the war, Squadron Leader L H Trent was subsequently decorated with the Victoria Cross, the highest British decoration, for his bravery during this mission.

German Invasion Barges being prepared on French coast

New Roles

In 1944 the first North American P.57 Mustangs were delivered to R.A.F. Leiston in Suffolk. Because these aircraft had far longer range the previous role of meeting the bombers on their way back from missions was extended. They were able to penetrate to Leipzig where the unit gained their first Distinguished Unit Citation and later they were used for dive-bombing and strafing strategic tragets such as airfields, marshalling yards and ammunition dumps.

Air Sea Rescue

Initially only at Martlesham Heath, but later at Coltishall, Horsham St Faiths and Bircham Newton, Air Sea Rescue units were set up to rescue precious aircrew who had crashed into the sea. They were usually equipped with Walrus amphibians and Boston or Lysander search aircraft. The Walrus would land on the sea to effect rescue, or if the conditions were too bad, drop dinghies or rafts, as did the Boston and Lysander, and circle overhead to lead rescue boats to the scene.

When the Americans became involved in 1942 they set about improving the search radio system by installing 'radio fixing' stations at Leiston and Sea Palling. These new stations were a source of mystery, especially to the local inhabitants, and many strange interpretations of the reason for their existence abounded.

In July, 1940, an aircrew abandoned their crippled bomber over the North Sea and took to their dinghy. Although a heavy sea was running W. O. Thomas Ormiston of Martlesham Heath landed on the sea and took the crew into his rescue plane. As the waves were riding so high he could not take off again and so he radioed for assistance – which eventually came in the form of gunboats. Taxiing his Walrus through the choppy seas he was eventually taken in tow by one of the gunboats. The tow had to be abandoned however, and it was not until next morning that the Walrus and her passengers were brought into Lowestoft harbour by a motor patrol boat. For his courage, fortitude and resource, Ormiston was awarded the D.F.C.

A Westland Lysander overflying an R.A.F rescue launch

Foes as well as friends received assistance. In May 1942 a coastal patrol squadron from Ludham encountered a German bomber over the North Sea. They attacked, scoring hits on the tail and cockpit before the plane burst into flames. The German crew baled out and Squadron Leader Haywood alerted the A.S.R. unit at Coltishall who arranged their rescue.

In January 1944 an American crew abandoned their B-17 twenty miles (32 kms) off the Dutch coast. A high speed launch from Great Yarmouth went to their aid, found their dinghy and picked them up. Due to bad weather conditions, their escort aircraft lost them and they were attacked by a Junkers 88. The boat sank and the coxswain was killed but the others were picked up by a second launch from Yarmouth. Two doctors from Martlesham Heath were flown out to tend the survivors.

The Douglas Boston III, used extensively for sea search

Observer Corps at work. An Observation Post, maintaining a close watch on cities and other strategic points during the war

The Observer Corps

A quiet but substantial contribution to the effort to keep the enemy at bay, the Observer Corps maintained a close watch on cities and strategic points during the war. Mounted in their look-out towers, or some vantage point, these men risked life and limb as they waited and watched for the enemy.

Additionally they had to identify, record and relay to the co-ordinating centres so that aeroplanes and other targets could be alerted. They were issued with identification codes and were afforded ample practice in the early months of the war by the multitude of craft flying over. Even when RADAR was widely used the Observer Corps were still needed to confirm the electronic signals, and to stand in when RADAR broke down.

Other Helpers

The Air Transport Auxiliary and the Air Training Corps gave invaluable assistance to the R.A.F. The A.T.A. employed many women and one of their jobs was to ferry planes from either manufacturer or repair depots to the operational airfields. Perhaps the most famous of these women was Amy Johnson, who was posted as missing on 5th January, 1941. The mystery of her death was solved on 3rd April, 1975, when the wreckage of her aircraft and her remains were found off Canvey Island.

An early opportunity for training, and a ripe field for recruitment, was the Air Training Corps, which was formed to give an insight and an early experience of the air forces. The Anti-Aircraft Command also played a great part in the defence of England by manning anti-aircraft guns, searchlight emplacements and the dispersal and raising of barrage balloons.

Another helper – a voluntary nursing auxiliary

Chain Home radar towers

RADAR

The idea of using radio signals bouncing off objects to give their range and size was born in 1934-35 and developed at Bawdsey Manor, near Orfordness. Leading research pioneers were Sir Robert Watson Watt, Professor John Cockroft and Mr. R. J. Dippy, and they extended the original ideas and perfected systems that were used by fighters and bombers. The first system was the C. H. (Chain Home) network which spread from the South coast to North Norfolk and their high towers were a constant menace to aircraft but they were very vulnerable to attack. Later it was found that it was more effective to beam radio signals from low aerials as the resulting narrow beam enabled more reliable and identifiable echoes.

A great step forward was made just before the war when Robert Watson Watt devised a system, I.F.F. (Identification Friend or Foe) by relaying signals which could be picked up by friendly aircraft and relayed back; an invaluable aid in later battles.

During the Battle of Britain the name was changed to Radio Detection and Ranging the resulting palindromic initials of RADAR being formed.

Early radio units were huge and costly, but by the early 40's smaller units were produced and fitted into ships and aircraft. Ground RADAR stations were built all over Eastern England.

As the Germans developed their own radar equipment, methods to jam them had to be devised. American Boeing Fortresses from Little Snoring, Foulsham, North Creake and Oulton were used to carry the heavy transmitting equipment needed for this jamming, whilst Stirlings and Halifaxes from Stradishall flew with loads of shredded silver paper which they released as 'Window' to confuse the German radar. Meanwhile the RADAR stations in East Anglia continued their valuable work watching and reporting the 'blips'.

Subterfuge

Often the Germans crossed the North Sea aiming to bomb and wreck the East Anglian airfields and thereby destroy the capability of the R.A.F. to defend and attack. Indeed many airfields were thus attacked but the effectiveness of these raids was lessened by the Decoy sites. These were set up at the side of the real airfields and were fitted with dummy equipment to confuse the enemy. Some sites were equipped with flare path lighting and decoy aircraft (manufactured by the film industry property men) whilst others had flare paths only. Also SD sites were introduced adjacent to large cities to give an idea of a built up area. Many of these sites were bombed on several occasions and certainly justified their existence.

Dummy aircraft and hangars

Invaluable counter attack measures were made available by the acquisition of German fighters and bombers. In September, 1941, there was great curiosity when a Heinkel III, a Junkers 88 and two Messerschmitts arrived at Duxford from Farnborough. Thereafter they were displayed at other stations.

When four Resistance Dutchmen required passage from Amsterdam they were to be picked up in September 1940 by a captured Fokker T8W seaplane as it was felt that this would not arouse the suspicion of the Germans in Holland. Accordingly plans were laid but weather prevented take-off on the first two nights. On the third, the Fokker took off only to be fired upon when it reached the rendezvous point. The old plane took off through searchlights and gunfire and safely reached Felixstowe again ... only to be fired upon by some over-enthusiastic Home Guard. It later transpired that the Dutch agents had been captured by the Germans on the second night and the ambush set for when the Fokker landed.

Foreign plane in British possession

Reconnaissance was a very important part of a fighter plane's duties. When a Junkers 88 landed at Oakington on 19th September, 1940, having been captured by two Hurricanes, it was found to contain many sophisticated German cameras. These were later adapted for use by reconnaissance Spitfires that had been painted in the grey-blue, whites and pinks used to blend with the sky. These Spitfires were supplemented by Mosquitos for night photography using high powered flashbulbs.

Gloster Meteor, the R.A.F.'s first jet fighter

New Ideas

Many new ideas for aeroplanes, bombing devices and techniques, defence strategies, etc., were worked out in Eastern England on airfields specially set aside for this type of work. One important development took place at Newmarket Heath field in December, 1941, when trials were carried out on the Gloster F9/40 which was to become the Gloster Meteor, the first and only allied jet aeroplane used in the war. Great secrecy was the order of the day for these trials and even R.A.F. personnel were kept away from the scene by service policemen.

Hitler's Secret Weapons – V1's, V2's and V3's

By 1942 intelligence reports told of a new range of secret weapons being developed by the Germans. These were pilotless bombs that were to be launched 24 hours a day against our cities.

The first type, known as the V1 was a 1800 lb (800 kg) bomb powered by a pulse jet engine whose distinctive guttural drone earned it the nickname "Doodlebug" or "Buzz Bomb". It was provided with just enough fuel to reach its target, over which the engine would stop and it would crash and explode. The navigational system used involved several gyro compasses. The R.A.F. found that the easiest way to destroy them was to fly alongside and tip them over by using the fighter's wing tip, thus upsetting the gyros and making the V1 crash.

THE 'V1' OR 'DOODLEBUG'

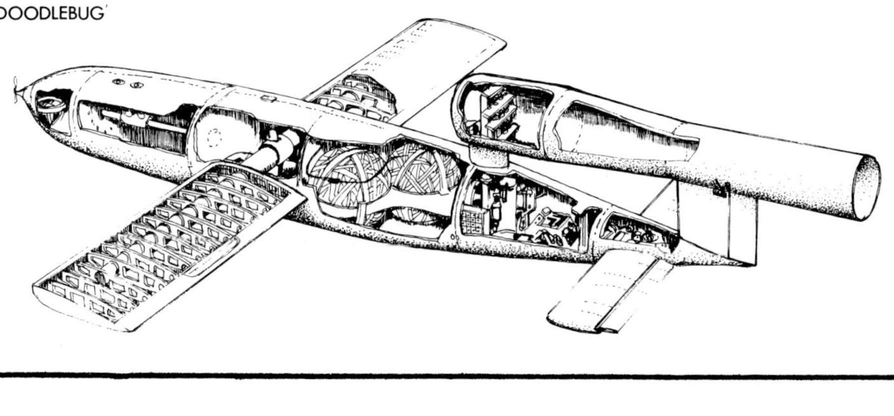

Although many reached targets in Britain, and escaped fighter interception, it was the relentless pounding of their launching sites by Allied bombers that saved Britain from an even more destructive onslaught.

Against the revolutionary V2, however, there was no defence. Powered by a single stage rocket motor, it reached heights and speeds beyond our tracking capabilities and interception was impossible. The V2 was much larger than the V1 and it carried a devastating warhead. No warning was given of its approach but the shock of its arrival was immense. It brought death, destruction and demoralisation. This rocket was developed by Wernner von Braun who later became one of America's foremost rocket experts, being involved in the Polaris missile project and the American space programmes.

The V3 rocket gun was a giant multi-barrelled weapon, designed to launch rocket propelled missiles, and constructed at a large underground site near Calais. This deadly weapon was capable of bombarding London with 600 tons of explosives per day. The project was abandoned after the Calais site was destroyed by bomber attack using 'Grand Slam' and'Tallboy' earthquake bombs, designed by Barnes Wallis

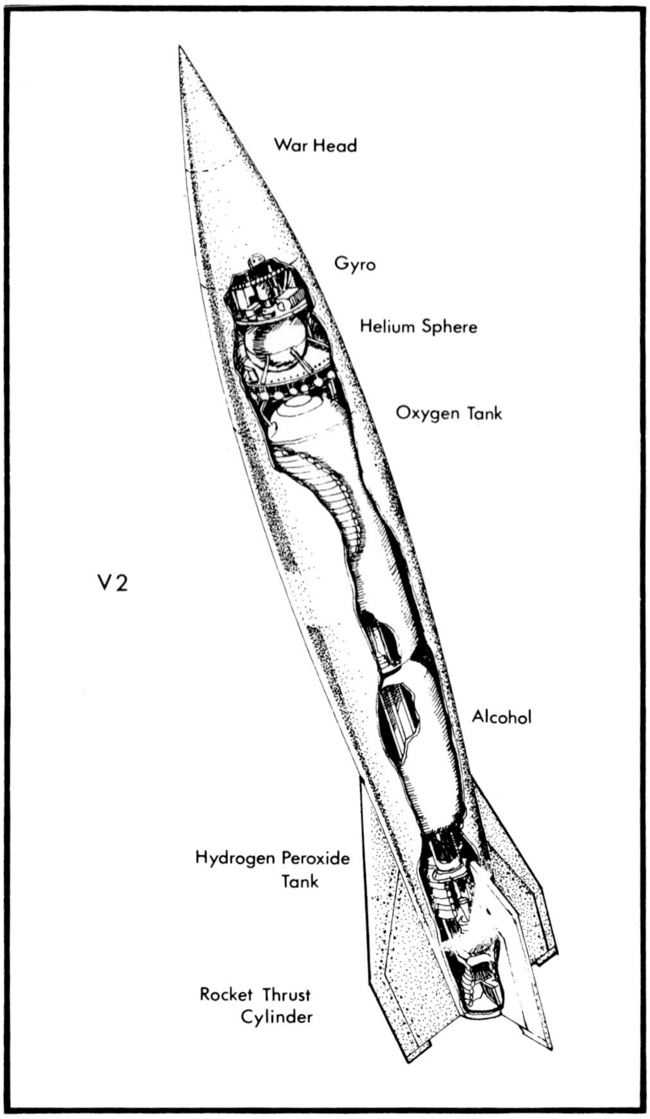

V2 Rocket

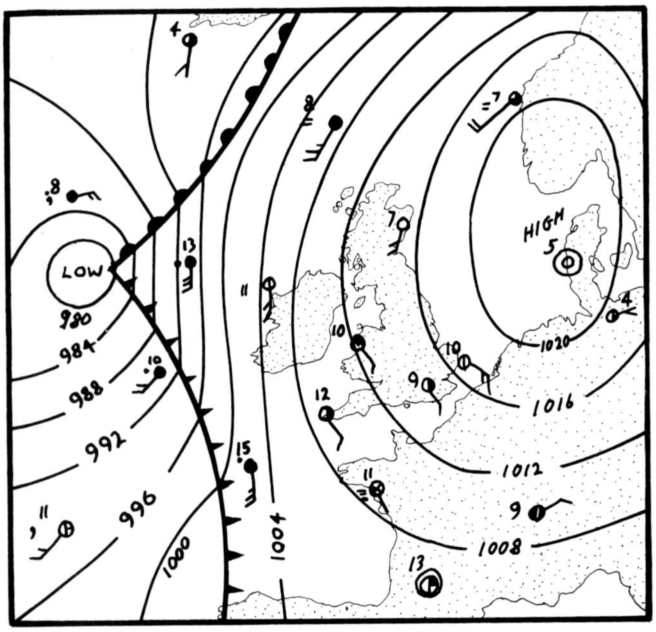

Typical weather chart

Meteorological Flights

Undramatic, but vital, the Meteorological Flights from Duxford and Bircham Newton flew in specially adapted Spitfires. Fitted with special instruments these pressurised and unarmed craft would fly to a height of 25,000 feet (7500 metres) and take readings and observe climatic conditions so that weather maps could be built up. Accurate forecasting was of great value to both bombers and fighters for raids had to be aborted in cases of low cloud, clear skies, etc. Previously the information had been gathered from shipping in the Atlantic but this source was denied during the war. It was vitally important to keep weather forecasts and information away from the enemy.

PLACES TO VISIT:

The Battle of Britain is celebrated annually during September. All over the country R.A.F. Stations are opened to the public and special flying displays and parades take place as the nation recalls how much "was owed by so many to so few".

Battle of Britain Memorial Flight
R.A.F. Coningsby, Nr Sleaford, Lincs — Telephone: 0526 44041

Here you can see, on permanent year-round exhibition, five Spitfires, the only remaining flying Lancaster and a Hurricane. The second Hurricane crash-landed at R.A.F. Wittering in September 1991, but hopefully it will be possible for this famous aircraft to fly again with its partner. During the summer months regular flying displays are advertised.

Coningsby is a front line fighter aircraft station whose Tornado aircraft saw action in the 1991 Gulf War.

Lincolnshire Aviation Heritage Centre
East Kirkby, Nr Spilsby, Lincs — Telephone: 07903 207

This Heritage Centre uses the former airfield of Five Group Bomber Command and the buildings have been restored to recreate the atmosphere of the early 1940's.

Imperial War Museum
Duxford Airfield
South of Cambridge on the M11 — Telephone: 0223 833963

Marvellous family day out with many things to do and see, and the finest collection of military and civil aircraft in the country. See inside the prototype Concorde and take the opportunity of taking to the skies yourself.

A Spitfire Mk1X PR, of the Battle of Britain Flight at R.A.F Coningsby, stripped down for servicing

Chapter 3. MISSION

Whilst Fighter Command was principally concerned with defending our island and attacking military targets in Western Europe, it was the bombers that struck at the heart of the enemy. Missions were flown to destroy strategic targets, thus wrecking the war effort and shattering the morale of the German people.

Capabilities of Principal Bombers 1939-45

Country	Type	Max. load	Max. range
Germany	Heinkel He 111	5,510 lbs	1,740 miles
	Dornier Do 217	8,818 lbs	1,500 miles
	Ju 88A-6	5,720 lbs	1,696 miles
	Heinkel He 177	14,400 lbs	2,795 miles
	Focke-Wulf FW-200	4,626 lbs	2,760 miles
Great Britain	Vickers Wellington	6,000 lbs	1,325 miles
	Short Stirling	14,000 lbs	1,930 miles
	Handley-Page Halifax	13,000 lbs	1,030 miles
	Avro Lancaster	22,000 lbs	1,660 miles
	D.H. Mosquito	4,000 lbs	1,370 miles
United States	Boeing B-17G	17,600 lbs	1,850 miles
	Boeing B-29	12,000 lbs	3,250 miles
	North American B-25 Mitchell	4,000 lbs	1,275 miles
	Consolidated B-24 Liberator	5,000 lbs	1,700 miles

RAF Bomber Sorties and Losses, 1939–45

Night sorties	297,663
Losses	7,449
Day sorties	66,851
Losses	876

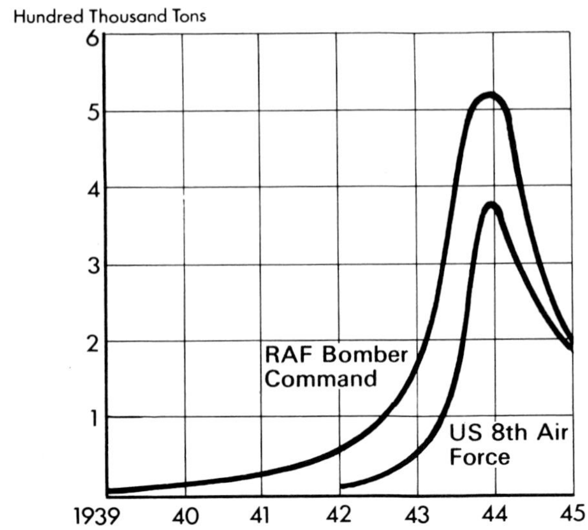

British and American Bomber Offensive against Germany, 1939-45

During the war years, thousands upon thousands of tons of high explosives were dropped on enemy territory, causing untold damage and killing countless numbers of people. This was the offensive aspect of the war. Certainly it was required of the fighting forces that our own land be defended, and certainly the best defence is attack. As to whether the destructive force of the bombers is justified in the long-term story of civilisation is a matter for history and for each of us to decide in our consciences. Our purpose is but to relate.

The R.A.F.

A Handley-Page Halifax bomber landing and being checked in. 6,176 of these were built for the R.A.F. between 1940 and 1946

Bomber Command Headquarters were at Uxbridge in Middlesex and at the beginning of the war, bombers in use were the Bristol Blenheims, the Vickers Wellingtons and the Handley Page Hampdens. Other types such as the Fairey Battle and Armstrong Whitworth Whitley, although out-classed and almost obsolete, still had parts to play until production from our bomber factories built up sufficient reserves to enable them to be withdrawn from operational flying and revert to training roles. Later the new heavy bombers, such as Short Stirlings, Handley Page Halifax's and Avro Lancasters would come into service delivering heavier bomb loads further and faster than ever before. All these planes operated from airfields in Eastern England during the war.

Kitted out to keep warm

As the aircraft were not the palatial heated machines they are today, special clothing had to be worn by the aircrew to combat the chilling cold. Generally speaking two different types of 'uniforms' were used, including the flying overalls shown in the photograph which had a separate heated zip-in lining. The main component of the other uniform was the Irwin flying jacket. All the flyers' wore sheepskin-lined boots and gloves and everything was of excellent quality, much prized by the crews. After the war, both jackets and boots were used by many motorcyclists and outdoor workers and, even today, one can still see advertisements offering R.A.F. pattern flying jackets. The helmets used had built-in ear-phones and intercommunication mouth piece, or 'mike', to enable the crew to keep in contact with each other.

For identification purposes, all aircraft had a serial number and letters which referred to the aircraft call sign and flight.

The number of airmen required to man a bomber varied according to the type and size of aircraft. A Lancaster generally had a crew of seven; a pilot, a co-pilot who doubled up as a flight engineer, a navigator, a rear turret gunner, a front gunner, a mid-upper gunner and a wireless operator.

Crews usually included both officers and enlisted men who formed tightly-knit groups and, often, life-long friendships. Theirs was a bond of shared danger and risk.

D' Lancaster crew of 103 Squadron, 1 Group Bomber Command, stationed at Elsham Wolds in Lincolnshire. The painted bombs on the side of the Lancaster indicate that she had completed 39 missions at this point

Perils of Bombing

Lancaster bomber of the Battle of Britain Memorial Flight

From 1939 until the early months of 1942 the principle targets for the British bombers were shipping, the defences of France, Holland and Belgium and central troop concentrations there. The belief was that if enemy forces were allowed to build up in Western Europe, separated from us only by the North Sea, Great Britain would inevitably be invaded.

Bomber Command's attacks on the strategic targets were, therefore, vital and succeeded in achieving their objective, but the price paid was a heavy one. The light and medium bombers sustained heavy losses.

By 1942 it was decided to appoint Air Marshall "Bomber" Harris as head of Bomber Command. Prime Minister Winston Churchill backed his policy of mass bombing of German towns, which would not only destroy the German war industry but also demoralise the public.

New British heavy bombers, which were now fitted with radio aids to help with navigation and bomb aiming, were also assisted by the formation of Pathfinder squadrons. Their purpose was to fly in front of the main bomber force and pinpoint the targets with coloured parachute flares. The Pathfinders were crewed by experienced pilots and navigators using even more sophisticated electronic aids, and for the first time night bombing became more accurate and effective.

Badge of the U.S.A.A.F. 20th Tactical Fighter Wing, based at Kings' Cliffe from 1943

America Goes to War

During the early months of 1942, America was preparing for the largest peaceful invasion the world had ever seen. The American Army Air Force, as it was then known, was gearing up to move into England to help the British armed forces in the struggle against Germany. The U.S.A. was drawn into the war when the Japanese attacked Pearl Harbour. East Anglia was to be the base for most of the Americans and their style of dress, mannerisms and pockets full of dollars soon led to mixed feelings of resentment and envy amongst our own armed forces. The saying went: "The only trouble with the Yanks is overdressed, overpaid and over here."

Unaccustomed to our reserved social habits, they blundered for a while but soon settled in. First came engineering units, working at fever pitch to build airbases from scratch, followed by bomber and fighter units. In strategy the American policy differed vastly from that of the R.A.F. They planned mass daylight raids at high altitude by bombers armed with many guns, flying in very tight formations that enabled mass gunfire to be brought to bear on any German fighters that tried to attack them. That was the theory, but in practice on the early raids many of these brave airmen lost their lives and this continued until they were provided with fighter escorts.

Operation Oyster

During September and October of 1942, Venturas, Mosquitos and Bostons took off from many East Anglian stations, striking military targets of all kinds over Europe. One such target was the Philips radio and electrical component factory at Eindhoven, where essential equipment was made for the German war effort. Of the many bombers involved in this raid, code-named 'Operation Oyster', were 30 Venturas from Feltwell bearing incendiary bombs.

So that they were not picked up by enemy radar they flew low over the sea and crossed the flat lands of Holland, arriving at Eindhoven on schedule. They bombed the factory and started a blaze which lit the whole city. 14 aircraft were lost, but this mission has gone down in the history of successful precision bombing raids on Europe.

Aerial view of target showing bomb damage

Special Delivery

One of the most unusual operations of the war began at Horsham St. Faiths in August, 1941, when a Blenheim bomber took off on a very special humane mission. Douglas Bader, the legless fighter pilot, had been shot down by enemy gunfire whilst on a strafing mission over occupied France. Whilst baling out of his stricken Spitfire, he lost one of his artificial legs, and after parachuting down to safety, was captured by the Germans and taken to a military hospital. A radio message was sent to England telling of his plight and asking if a spare leg could be sent. Thus the Blenheim crew flew to the hospital and dropped a leg by parachute to put our legless fighter ace back on his feet.

Blenheims ready for take off

Oilfields in Rumania

Fuel supplies are the life-blood of any country at war and without them the modern mechanised armies would soon grind to a halt. Thus oil installations were prime targets for the bombers on both sides of the conflict.

One such raid on the Ploesti oilfields in Rumania entailed flying across enemy-held territory for long distances to reach the targets and then coming down for a low-level attack. Most oil installations were well-defended by anti-aircraft guns and fighter stations; the Ploesti target was no exception.

A number of American Liberator bombers were hit approaching the target, and one flown by Second Lieutenant Lloyd Hughes, although badly damaged and streaming petrol, carried on to the target and bombed accurately. On the journey home he crashed and all his crew perished. Two other Liberator pilots from Hardwick, Lt. Col. Addison Baker and co-pilot Major John Jerstad, flying the lead plane, were also badly injured by German fighters but, undaunted, pressed on only to crash in the target area. Along with Second Lieutenant Hughes both these brave airmen were awarded their nation's homage in the form of the Medal of Honor.

Peenemunde

British Intelligence reports filtering through told of new pilotless bombers being developed by Germany at a top secret works at Peenemunde. This target was given top priority by the planners in London and, accordingly, on 17th August 1943, a force of 600 bombers from many East Anglian bases, under the control of Wing Commander J. H. Searby from Wyton, took off. The raid was a complete success, the works being totally destroyed, but 40 bombers were shot down by enemy gunfire and a further 15 crashed on the return journey.

Liberator Bomber flown by the U.S.A.A.F., from the photographic collection of Mr Tony North of Norwich.

Joseph Kennedy

The Americans were involved in the task of ridding the skies of the menace of the V rockets and part of their job was to destroy the actual sites from which the rockets were fired. They devised the plan of stripping a Liberator of all its internal fittings, packing it with high explosives, installing instruments which would allow it to be flown by remote controls operated by an accompanying aircraft, and exploding the doomed aircraft on the target. To ensure safe passage over England two pilots would fly the Liberator bomb before ejecting over the Channel.

Joseph Kennedy

On Saturday, 12th August, the Liberator took off from Fersfield, flown by Lieutenant Joseph Kennedy (elder brother of the late U.S. President, John F. Kennedy) and Lieutenant Wilford Willy. Their target was the rocket base at Mimoyesques and as they were passing over Blythburgh, Kennedy was to test the controls of the robot pilot and before doing so, radioed his intention to the accompanying craft. The pilot of this craft gave the go-ahead and, seconds later, was shocked when, as Kennedy flicked the switch, his Liberator exploded in a flash of flame and smoke. Wreckage was scattered over a wide area of Suffolk countryside below.

Mass Raids

Following the first 1000 bomber raid on Cologne in May 1942, the success of this mission was expressed in several ways; only 39 bombers failed to return, the city was almost totally obliterated, 900 crews claimed to have hit the target and 1455 tons (tonnes) of bombs were dropped. A second mass raid against Essen a week later was only a partial success, due to low cloud obscuring the target. Later in May another 1000 bombers attacked Bremen with great success, even though 49 aircraft were destroyed and 64 damaged.

Bombers from all over Eastern England featured in these raids. There are records of Wellingtons taking off from Coningsby, Feltwell, Gt. Massingham, Oakington, Scampton and Waterbeach as well as from many other fields. The official objective was always some strategic target that lay within a city but the whole city was bombed and the damage done to German morale by the wholesale killing of civilians was considerable.

The Vickers' Wellington bomber – a most formidable machine which, due to its geodetic airframe design, was almost indestructible

American Daylight Missions

A typical raid was on the Focke Wolfe aircraft works at Bremen in April,1943. 107 bombers from East Anglia blasted this target but at what a cost: 15 bombers were destroyed and 48 damaged. Another raid that August highlights the determination of the Americans when, for the first time, they flew deep into the heart of Germany to attack the Ball Bearing Works at Schweinfurt. 363 B17's were involved and losses were high; 59 shot down and 57 badly damaged. Undeterred, within a month they returned to Schweinfurt, but again then German defences took a heavy toll. Of 291 bombers sent, 60 were shot down and 138 were damaged. This was to be the last long range daylight attack until fighter escorts could be provided.

Memorial at R.A.F. Kings' Cliffe near Peterborough, portraying Mustang (U.S.A.A.F.) and Spitfire wings. Incorporates U.S., Commonwealth and R.A.F. Squadron badges

The Dam Busters

When a new top secret unit known as X Squadron was formed at Scampton in March 1943 and Guy Gibson was posted in as commander, people wondered what was going on. Soon to be allocated a brand new squadron, No. 617, this was to become one of the most famous units of the war because of one raid that caught the imagination of the public – "The Dam Busters". Using specially modified Lancaster bombers to carry the revolutionary bouncing bomb, which was designed by Barnes Wallis, on May 17th, 1943 they raided and breached the Mohne and Eder dams in the Ruhr Valley, thus releasing millions of gallons of water that was stored in reservoirs for use in Hydro Electric power stations and industry. For his gallant leadership in this raid, Guy Gibson was awarded the Victoria Cross, Britain's highest award for bravery.

Guy Gibson, Commander, 617 Squadron: the Dam Busters

617 Squadron was especially formed for this one mission, but due to its success, a decision was made to utilise it as a special operations unit. Later they hit the headlines again when they sank the German battleship Tirpitz on 2nd November, 1944, by using more specialised bombs developed by Barnes Wallis. Professor Wallis was one of the greatest military inventors of his time. His "Tallboy" weighing 12,000 lbs (5500 kilo's) and "Grand Slam", weighing 22,000 lbs (10,000 kilo's), were outsized streamline darts that passed the speed of sound as they dropped. They were designed to penetrate deep into the ground and then explode, thus creating an earthquake effect to destroy the target. Barnes Wallis promised that a near miss would be as effective as a direct hit and this prediction was proved to be correct when the important Bielfefeld Viaduct was destroyed by using this method. These bombs were also used with great effect against U Boat bases and flying bomb sites, targets that were previously impregnable.

Dropping Troops

In early 1944, residents of the Thetford area were mystified by the curious movement of aircraft overhead, for in addition to much movement during the days, there was the flare dropping at night and simulated air attacks. This was in preparation for the D Day Landings on 6th June, when aircraft of all types were assisting in the Allied Landings in Normandy. Records show that practically all operational stations flew missions of various kinds on that day. Following the meteorological flights from Bircham Newton, Wyton and Wattisham, fighters flew from Duxford, Coltishall, West Raynham, Leiston, Steeple Morden, Halesworth, Fowlmere and Wattisham. The fighters were to escort the bomber support from Tibenham, Seething, Glatton, East Wretham, Thorpe Abbott, Shipdham, Bourn, Swannington, and Horsham St. Faiths, for the soldiers landing on the beaches. These missions went on through the day and night and there was no respite from the deafening roar of the aircraft.

«HORSA GLIDER»

The inhabitants of Eastern England were treated to a further rare show of strength three months later when during the 16th to the 18th of September, some 1,500 aircraft assembled. Their task was to tow Horsa gliders filled with troops and Hamilcar gliders carrying tanks and other transport over the North Sea to take part in the Arnhem landings. When over the target the troop carrying planes disgorged their airborne parachutists whilst the gliders detached themselves from their tugs to land their fighting forces at ground level. Aircraft flying in this mission came from the south of England mainly but fighters and support bombers came from Hardwick, East Wretham and Coltishall.

Gliders and bombers at Woodbridge waiting to take off

A mysterious station was Somersham, where the occasional Hudson or Lysander were seen. Usually at night and with the minimum of personnel, these aircraft took off and returned some hours later. The story is that they were used to ferry Resistance fighters and underground agents.

To Confuse and Undermine

Steeple Morden in Cambridgeshire was nothing but a satellite station for Bassingbourn but several events took place which convinced the locals that it was really a top secret base with all its buildings hidden underground! It served to confuse the enemy also for in February 1940 the Germans were involved in an air raid on Birmingham and a Junkers 88 crew, completely lost on a cloudy night, thought that they were over occupied France when they saw Steeple Morden in the moonlight. They landed and were amazed when a Blenheim attacked them. They fired signal cartridges and slewed across the runway, badly damaging their plane. The four crewmen were captured and parts from the craft, which was too badly damaged to repair, were used to renew other Junkers 88's held by the British.

An operation which could be considered an approved practical joke, but really had a serious motive, was that planned by the Free Frenchman, Sir Philip Joubert de la Ferte, who was Air Officer Commanding Coastal Command. In 1942 British morale was mounting, but with continued German presence in France, an effort was needed to raise the French morale. In order to do this it was planned to roar down the Champs-Elysées in the middle of a daily German parade there and drape the French flag over the Arc de Triomphe.

Flight Lieutenant A. K. Gatward and Sergeant Fern were detailed with this assignment on 13th May 1942 but bad weather delayed the attempt until 12th June. On that day, of all days, the Germans held no parade, but undaunted, the Beaufighter flew up the Champs-Elysées and planted the flag as planned. The crew, to make up for the lack of the parade, shot up the top floor of the Gestapo Headquarters in Paris before returning home at low level to avoid radar. The French were uplifted by this event and the chagrin of the Germans was not covered by their official statement that a "Luftwaffe plane had flown out of control"!

A patriotic Arc de Triomphe

Heroism

In both fighters and bombers the Allied and German forces flew routinely dangerous operations and occasionally rose to heroism 'beyond the call of duty'. Beyond instinct, beyond patriotism, there were events that eloquently tell of self-sacrifice and tremendous courage.

On the night of 12th August 1943 a squadron of Stirlings flew from Downham Market airfield to bomb the Fiat works in Turin. These raids were always dangerous for in addition to the long distance there were the Alps to negotiate on the return. 218 Squadron bombed the Fiat works successfully but over the target one plane, flown by Flight Sergeant Louis Aaron, was machine gunned and three engines were knocked out, the control cables were damaged and the cockpit was raked, mortally wounding the pilot. It was quickly decided to head for Africa as negotiation of the Alps was out of the question because a bomb aimer had to fly the plane taking written instructions from Aaron, who was in such terrible pain that he just could not handle the craft. Bone airport was sighted after five hours flying and the plane was landed at the fifth attempt with the pilot assisting as much as he could, although on the verge of collapse. On arrival he was rushed to hospital but died there nine hours later. Flight Sergeant Aaron was awarded a posthumous V.C. for his courage.

On a November raid on the Fiat works in Turin, one of the planes was piloted by an Australian, Sergeant Middleton, who was stationed at Lakenheath. Middleton's plane bombed its target but was then hit by flak which struck the wing and the cockpit injuring both pilots. Middleton lost the sight of his right eye but he ordered the second pilot to receive treatment whilst he continued to fly the plane. The plane made it through the Alps on the way home but was again hit by flak whilst crossing the French coast. Most of the crew baled out over the channel before the plane crashed into the sea killing the three on board. Middletons' body was recovered the next day and was taken to Beck Row to be buried, having been awarded a posthumous V.C.

Aerial view of Woodbridge

The Americans too exhibited a selfless brand of valour and daring. On the afternoon of 25th June, R.A.F. fighter crews waiting to scramble at Coltishall jumped from their seats in anticipation, as a crippled Flying Fortress lumberingly circled the airfield, its crew one by one parachuting out. They rushed to pick up the Americans as the plane headed away from the field and they were told that the pilot could not land as the undercarriage was hopelessly damaged. Rather than risk the runway he flew out to sea over Waxham and ditched his plane after baling out.

A similar incident happened on 23rd September, 1944 at Woodbridge. An American B24 Liberator bomber from Attlebridge was badly damaged and could not be landed. The pilot ordered his crew to bale out, headed the stricken machine out over the coastline to crash into the sea and parachuted out himself. Instead of heading out to sea, the unmanned aircraft turned and flew over the airfield for ten minutes at full power, performing the most amazing stalls and side slips. Eventually the tail unit broke away and fell into the scrapyard at Woodbridge, and the main section, with engines still screaming, dived onto the runway half burying itself in the concrete!

On 9th November, 1944, a squadron of Flying Fortresses, piloted by young G.I.'s, took off to bomb a target in France. As they entered the target area the craft flown by First Lieutenant Donald J. Gott and Second Lieutenant William E. Metzger was soundly hit by flak which put three of its engines out of action and set fire to the fuselage. Wheeling away from the target Gott clung to the controls of the blazing plane. The crew, who had escaped injury, parachuted out, leaving Gott and Metzger to bring three wounded comrades down. As the plane came in to land it exploded in a ball of flame which killed all on board. For their gallantry the two pilots were awarded the Medal of Honour, the U.S. equivalent of the V.C.

Flying Fortress dropping bombs

Fighter Cover for the Bombers

By 1944 the long range fighters were available to escort our bombers to the target and back on daylight raids. The P47 Thunderbolt and P51 Mustang, and the twin-fuselage P38 Lightning all fitted with long range drop tanks to extend their range, gave protection from base to target. Their special fuel tanks could be jettisoned in flight, should the enemy fighters appear, and they could then attack on equal terms. These planes were also adapted for night fighting and flew with the bombers seeking out the German fighters. Thus the hunter became the hunted. Instead of prowling among our night bombers, picking off targets at will, the Germans were now the victims, becoming less and less willing to get involved.

The only bright star on the Luftwaffe horizon at this stage was the entry into service of the Messerschmitt 262A jet engined fighter, with a maximum speed of 528 m.p.h. (845 kmh). No allied aircraft could match its speed but its range and handling aspects were not good and the most important factor from our bomber crews point of view was that it was not available in large numbers.

The British Gloster Meteor jet had first flown in 1943 and was the only jet aircraft to enter service with the R.A.F. during World War II.

American War Cemetery at Madingley

On a site donated by Cambridge University, at Madingley close to Cambridge, is built one of the most beautiful memorials erected by any country to honour its dead. No visitor can fail to be moved by its serene simplicity, or fail to recall that the men buried here gave their lives helping to defend England against the horrors of occupation.

The buildings and crosses are dedicated to the 5,125 missing Americans as well as the ones that were once, or still are, buried here. A visit is recommended to remind us all of the enormous sacrifices made by Americans during the Second World War.

The American War Cemetery at Madingley, Cambridge

Commonwealth Squadrons and Other Volunteers

This chapter would be incomplete without mentioning the volunteers from Europe and the Commonwealth squadrons.

With the outbreak of war in 1939 the ranks of the R.A.F. were swollen by many volunteers from countries not directly involved in the struggle, like Jews from Palestine who wanted to fight the Germans. Others, having seen their homelands overrun by the Nazis, fled to England and joined our forces to fight again. Polish, Free French, Dutch and Belgians were just a few of those who fought with a personal vengeance that, to some, was difficult to understand. They had been driven from their homelands by an enemy that put no value on civilian life and not knowing whether their loved ones were alive or in concentration camps. They did not dare to try and communicate in case of reprisals against family and friends in countries still under German occupation. The only way they could vent their feelings was to get back into action, and the exploits of these men alone could fill several volumes.

Typical of war-time posters

The Commonwealth supplied many trained pilots as well as engineers and other trades. Squadrons from Canada, Australia, New Zealand, Rhodesia and South Africa, to mention but a few, often flew together as crews in bombers attached to normal R.A.F. units.

Within the first few months many Americans, too, crossed the Atlantic to fight against the enemy and later, in 1942, when America entered the war, many of them preferred to stay with the R.A.F. and not join the American Air Force, although their pay, uniform and conditions in general were better.

Perhaps the largest compliment we can pay these brave airmen is to just take a few lines from the record books of the scores (number of enemy aircraft shot down) of fighter aces during the Second World War. Topping the list are:-

1. Sqdn. Ldr. M. T. Pattle, D.F.C. and Bar, South Africa	38 victories
3. Gp. Capt. A.G. (Sailor) Malan, D.S.O. and Bar, D.F.C. and Bar, South Africa	35 victories
4. Sqdn. Ldr. P. H. Clostermann, D.F.C. and Bar, French	33 victories
5. Wg. Cdr. B.E. Finucane, D.S.O., D.F.C. and 2 bars, Irish	32 victories
6. Sqdn. Ldr. G. F. Beurling, D.S.O., D.F.C., D.F.M. and Bar, Canadian	31 victories

V.E. Day

On 9th May 1945 the Germans surrendered to the Allied forçes and suddenly the war was over.

The planes were stilled and Allies and Germans alike counted their dead and injured: in Britain some 60,595 civilians were killed and 86,182 were severly injured in air-raids, and the Allied Forces were responsible for the deaths of 597,623 Germans.

As part of the V.E. Day celebrations, bonfires were lit throughout the land. This 'Guy' was to burn on the beach at Wells in Norfolk

Typical scene in an officers' mess

Chapter 4. OFF DUTY

The custom in the Armed Forces was that officers and other ranks did not mix during off duty hours. This stems from the segregation on camp where the officers, senior N.C.O.s, junior N.C.O.s and other ranks all had different dining, recreation and sleeping quarters. Within the bomber crews, however, it was not uncommon for the skipper to be a non-commissioned officer with commissioned officers in his crew. Drawn together by the dangerous nature of their work, they formed very tightly-knit groups and preferred each others company but had to meet off camp for drinking, dancing and other social functions.

A favoured method of getting from A to B on the ground – the motor-bike, often fuelled by illegal green petrol

Most of the men who kept the enemy at bay, or flew in missions over enemy territory, were young, and therefore able to withstand a certain amount of stress and strain. Because of the inhuman pressure exerted by flying, allied to a natural youthful exuberance, it went without saying that any excuse was used for them to let off steam. They would celebrate anything, including successful missions, nursing damaged bombers back home, and birthdays, as if every party would be the last, and often it was. The romanticism associated with the uniformed 'Boys in Blue', 'Brylcreem Boys' and the G.I.s has lasted over 40 years, and stories of their antics still circulate today.

Public Houses

A favourite haunt of the airmen in the Coltishall area was the Ferry Inn at Horning. This was a low, thatched building nestling at the end of the un-made up lane alongside the River Bure. It became the scene of dances and socials and was a romantic meeting place for Air Force personnel and the local inhabitants. Regular dances were held in the club room and, naturally, in such a secluded place, activities became rather wild, and people became careless of accepted safety procedures. A dance was held on the evening of April 20th, 1941, and it is said that blackout measures were not implemented fully. A lone bomber, somewhat off course from a raid on nearby Norwich, dropped a stick of bombs. With no warning having been given, the revellers had no opportunity to escape and twenty-two people were killed, including three pilots from Coltishall, and many others were injured. Such was the scene of devastation next morning that no attempt was made to recover the bodies, and the site was levelled with bulldozers. The Ferry Inn was subsequently rebuilt on the same spot and there is a commemorative plaque on the wall in the bar.

A local public house, close to an airfield, often became the haunt of the crews of the aeroplanes who were anxious to get out of the confines of the camp. Here the local people got to know and respect the airmen and tolerated their bursts of exuberance that often spilled outside the hostelry. A popular meeting-place was the Three Horseshoes at Scottow. A Spitfire propellor is fastened to the outside wall and the lounge is lined with photographs of airmen and aeroplanes of the 1939-45 era. Silenced by sepia, the planes and men pictured there made their mark during the war and reference to them unleashes a fund of stories.

The Three Horseshoes at Scottow

There was the crew that came in after a mission, passed a five-pound note over the counter and proceeded to spend the evening drinking and laughing, as usual. At closing time many watched anxiously as the four men left in a rather stumbling fashion to return to the airfield at Coltishall in an Austin Ten. Nothing was heard of them again because their plane was shot down the following day.

Daredevil Pranks

The airmen in their off-duty hours would often seek some dare, or practical joke to take their thoughts away from the mind-bending and perilous task of flying over enemy territory. Their dares involved feats of strength or courage, usually featured cars or motorcycles, and were often dangerous. Our off-duty airmen rarely discussed their missions, but they regularly bragged about their pranks.

Extra-curricular Activities

On one of the searchlight bases near a certain Lincolnshire airfield, the crews often had time to spare but little money and few facilities to use it to the full. And so they would supplement their paltry earnings with the cash derived from catching and selling rabbits, which were valuable on account of the meat shortage. Imagine their delight when they shot and killed a fully grown deer! Half afraid of the possible reaction, they took the joints which they had cut from the carcase to the butcher's shop; their fears were groundless, for the venison was welcomed as 'beef' and the searchlight crew were well rewarded.

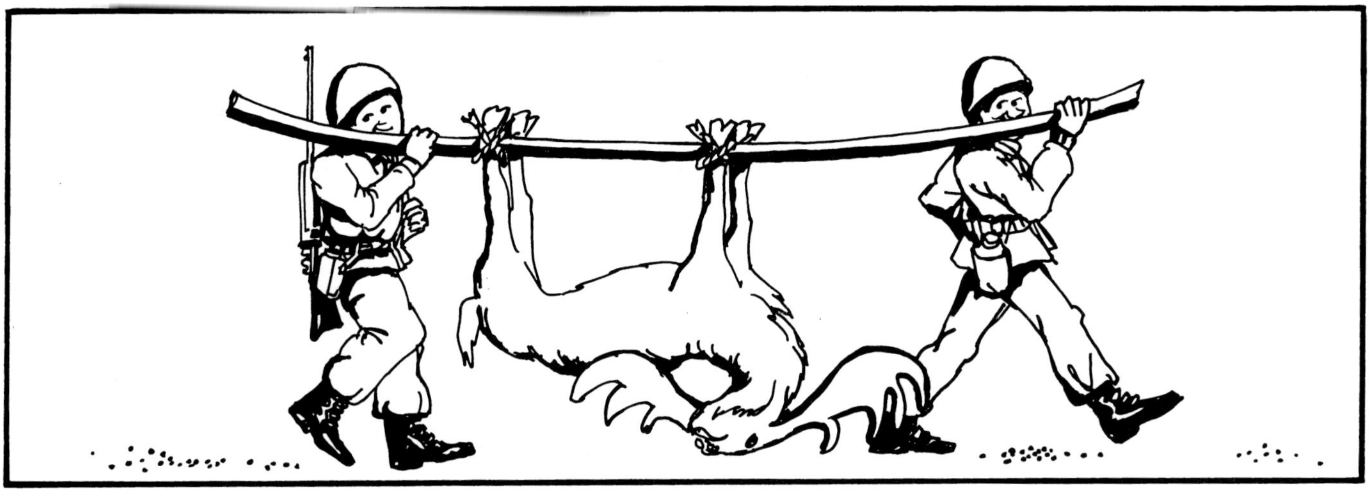

Cycles were extremely scarce and expensive and the hiring out of them was a lucrative business as Fred Dodger of Chapel Street, Norwich, found out. The Americans in particular took great delight in hiring old-fashioned cycles from him and riding up and down the street, much to the delight of the residents.

When four airmen from a base in South Norfolk stated their intention of going to Norwich to buy a bicycle each it was thought that they would be extremely lucky to get one. Their room mates had great difficulty in believing their story that, having successfully bought the cycles and stopped for a well-earned drink at a nearby public house, the cycles were stolen from against the wall where they had left them!

The Americans

On 10th October, 1942, a U.S.A.A.F. Liberator flew into Shipdam bringing the first Americans to Eastern England. They flew from our airfields alongside the R.A.F. and a certain amount of friction became apparent between them and the British airmen. The "G.I.s" (slang for General Issue), morale sky-high, well-equipped with some of the best aircraft in the world, had only one thing lacking and that was combat experience. Our aircrews, veterans of perhaps the Battle of Britain or a number of night-bombing missions over Germany, resented being told how easy it was going to be to bomb Germany into submission, in daylight too! Later events proved how wrong the U.S.A.A.F. tactics were. The daylight bombing runs, without escort, proved to be disastrous and the Americans suffered terrible losses. Selected crews flew with the R.A.F. on night bombing raids, even though their crews were not trained for night-bombing and their aircraft were not designed for it. Terrible navigational errors scattered them all over Europe and when they returned to the British Isles it was to land at any airfield with a runway.

One crew, returning to a Suffolk public house after an absence of several days, related the story of their first night-bombing mission. Due to cloud they were separated from the main bomber force about an hour away from the target! They decided to go it alone but never found the pathfinder flares and while stooging around looking they were attacked by night fighters. Jettisoning their bomb load they escaped back into the clouds and set course for home. Eventually, they spotted a coastline, and followed it, only to find that they were over Ireland! No doubt a little embarrassed they turned due east, landed somewhere in Scotland and ran out of fuel just after touchdown! After getting their damaged bomber repaired they were able to return to Suffolk and tell their tale. An R.A.F. navigator suggested that the next time they flew a night mission they tied a reel of cotton to the bomber tail then they could find their way home at least!

To be fair to the yanks, many R.A.F. crews at the start of night-bombing missions could relate even worse tales of navigational misfortune.

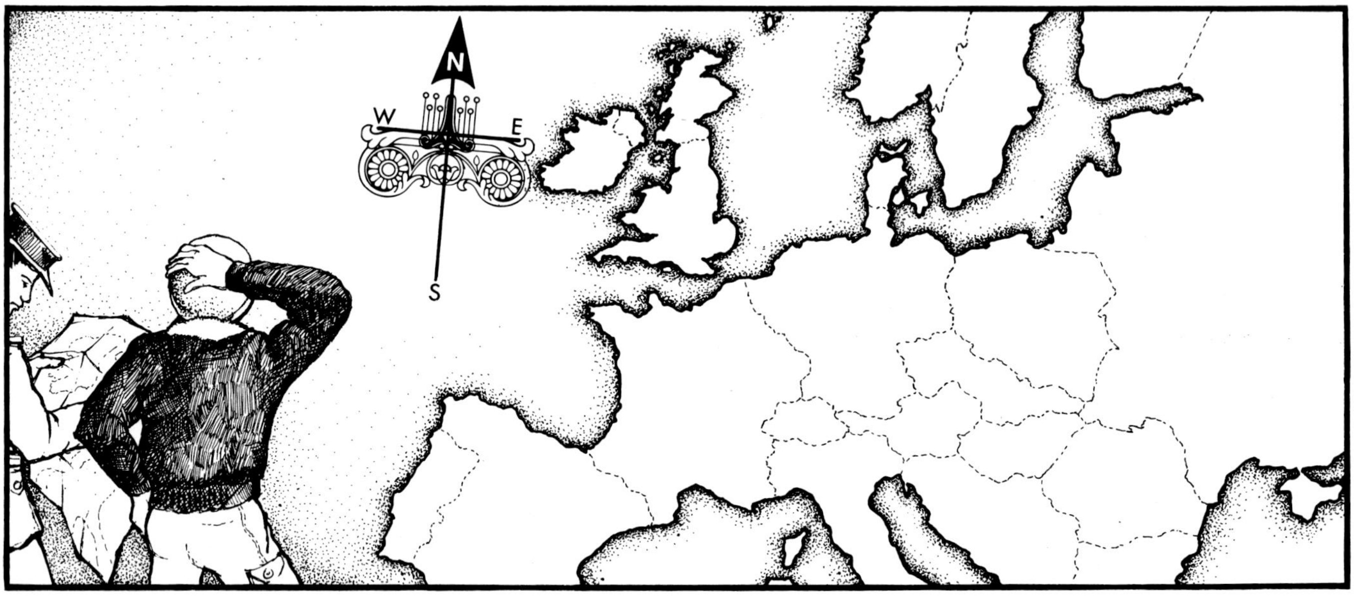

A small booklet called "BRITAIN" was issued by the U.S.A.A.F. to all G.I.s who were to spend some time here. Its purpose was to help integrate the young Americans.
'Be friendly, but don't intrude if it seems you are not wanted.'
'You are paid higher than the British. Don't rub it in. Play fair with him. He can be a pal in need.'
'Don't make fun of British speech or accents. You sound just as funny to them, but they are too polite to show it.'
'Never criticise the King or Queen.'
are some extracts from the booklet.

But the Americans can hardly have studied the booklet very closely for they aroused the admiration and passions of the young ladies and the resentment and anger of men and older ladies with their money, promiscuity and boasting. For instance, a story is told of a young G.I. who, having followed a 'young lady', at last called out, "Hi babe!" When she turned the young American saw that she was a very respectable old lady, and desperately blurted out, "Sorry, ma'am. I thought you were my mother." It did not go down too well.

The Americans were unfailingly outgoing and friendly and eventually were accepted into the hearts and homes of the East Anglians. On arrival at peoples' homes their pockets would be emptied and there were gifts for all the family. It was undoubtedly the generosity of the Americans that broke down social barriers and led to their acceptance.

Boeing B29, Superfortress, used extensively by the Americans towards the end of the war. This aeroplane is on its way to the Imperial War Museum at Duxford

It was not just their generosity that was found attractive, and this was proved when they eventually left, taking some 50,000 war brides with them, much to the chagrin of the British boys.

Waitresses in the better hotels who were not used to more than a muttered 'thank you' were invited to have a drink, and it could be said that the Americans started the easing of rigid social customs that had gone unaltered for ages. They were mystified by our drink licencing laws, amazed by our unarmed village bobby on his bicycle, and unable to understand why orderly queues were formed outside shops and at bus stops.

Local children were instructed in the art of baseball and American football and the G.I. would always have candy or chewing gum for the youngsters. The cry would follow them as they walked down the street–"Got any gum chum?"

Although usually well behaved and polite, at times American tempers frayed and fights occurred outside public houses and dance halls. The American Service Police, known as "Snowdrops" because of the white helmets worn, were soon at the scene and acted with ruthless indifference, cracking skulls with their clubs. The unconscious G.I.s were handcuffed and tossed into the ever-present jeep for their return to camp.

'Snowdrops' – American Military Policemen

Famous Americans

The image of the G.I.s, smart and casual in their 'pinks', armed with stuffed wallets and wads of chewing gum, and with a glowing reputation for amorous episodes, was enhanced by the occasional "great name" who came to Eastern England. A face or character who had previously only been known in lights or in the cast list of a film was suddenly 'over here'.

Perhaps the one who had the greatest impact, because of his long stay, was Captain James Stewart of the slow, laconic drawl and Western reputation. He was Group Executive Officer at Tibenham, Hardwick and Old Buckenham, and proved to be as shy and diffident in real life as he was in his film characterisations.

Glenn Miller and his famous band sometimes played at dances staged by the U.S.A.A.F., and organised by Captain Stewart. There are numerous girls who have spoken of their wartime romances which began in the heady atmosphere of the Glenn Miller sound. The Glenn Miller magic lives on and his music is still played today.

James Stewart

Glenn Miller

PLACES TO VISIT:
Neward Air Museum The Airfield, Winthorpe
Just off A46 from Lincoln,
Bombers such as the Halifax, Lancaster and Stirling were based at R.A.F. Winthorpe during World War II and some of these aircraft are on display. There are many other exhibits including a collection of aviation memorabilia. Open from April to October.

Norfolk & Suffolk Aviation Museum
Flixton, Nr Bungay,
Suffolk
A Member of the British Aircraft Preservation Society, a number of marvellous exhibits are on display. Open from April to October.

100th Bomb Group Memorial Museum,
Common Road Thorpe Abbotts, Dickleburgh,
Norfolk.
The Museum of memorabilia is housed in the original World War II control tower which has been restored by enthusiasts to commemorate U.S.A.F.'s 'Mighty Eighth'.

Chapter 5. TOUCHDOWN AND TECHNOLOGY

Rundown of the Fields

Derelict control tower near Sleaford in Lincolnshire.

And suddenly the war was over ....

With V.E. Day on 8th May 1945 the necessity for operations ceased and there was just no further need for the vast majority of airfields. Thus the aeroplanes were either put into storage or flown off to the Pacific to help the Americans deliver the last blow against the Japanese. Many of the R.A.F. personnel were kept on standby but most were demobilised so that they could renew vital civilian occupations, and some pilots joined civil airlines. And so the almost constant drone of the aeroplanes ceased, the air raid sirens were heard no more, the R.A.F. boys were gone and village dances and socials petered out due to lack of support.

In 1946, because of the attitude of the Soviets over the dividing up of Germany and especially of the capital, Berlin, it became necessary to get life-saving supplies to the people of West Berlin. This operation, known as the Berlin Airlift, started with eight aeroplanes working from Cambridge. The R.A.F. and U.S.A.A.F. were involved but much of the work went to 'sky tramps' – one of whom was later to become quite famous. Freddie Laker had bought a number of Halifax's for this purpose and operated them out of Southend airport.

After the airlift many of the remaining R.A.F. 'planes were sold off, some to overseas airforces, others to entrepreneurs like Freddie Laker and some were chartered out from small airfields by people like Billy Butlin who sold 'joy flights'. Yet more were sold for scrap and melted down on site and made into aluminium ingots, or bricks, which would later be turned into saucepans, a reversal of the early war years when households contributed saucepans to be made into airframes.

Handley Page Hastings; one of the types of 'plane used for the Berlin Airlift.

Back to Farming

The majority of stations in Eastern England closed for flying straight away and the stores and equipment moved out. The land was farmed for a time by the War Agricultural Committee (WAR.AG) before being re-possessed by its previous owners. Working parties moved in to take down the buildings and pull up the runways to be used as building materials to meet the postwar demand for housing. Apart from a few buildings and a landscape denuded of hedges, little trace of the airfields was left. In the cases where the land had been bought, it was usually possible for the previous owners to buy it back.

In August 1990 an exciting 'find' was made by the Bomber Airfield Society which triggered off Operation Merlin. Close to an airfield in what is now South Humberside, near Brigg, underneath a wheatfield, lay six perfectly preserved Lancaster bombers. The Society had heard from locals that just after peace was declared in 1945 six Lancasters had disappeared. They carried out reconnaissance flights over the area, and aerial photographs revealed two man-made hollows. Using a 'moon buggy' style piece of radar-photography equipment, the Lancasters, plus a Hamilcar glider, and packing cases containing spare parts and whole engines, were discovered. Why were they put there? Perhaps all will be revealed when the formidably expensive excavations begin.

Few visible traces there may have been but under the ground it was a different story. At U.S.A.A.F. Kings Cliffe, in Northamptonshire, a mass burial took place of spare parts, bicycles, portable buildings, vehicles and other sundry items. Heavy vehicles were used to run over all of these things to ensure that they were damaged beyond repair before burying them in massive pits. The reason given? To avoid flooding the market and thus damaging our local economy. Exactly the opposite logic to that used by the R.A.F. when they sold off surplus equipment, clothing and vehicles.

Three Drill Instructors. They trained National Service Airmen

Sale and Mothballs

Some stations, such as Little Snoring, Oulton and North Creake, were used to store the planes, transport and supplies removed from other stations. These fields were a scene of great activity as equipment was moved in and arrangements made for the regular sale of surplus equipment. The goods were quickly bought up by the locals who had felt the loss and shortage of clothing, transport and furniture which was a result of the previous single-minded war effort.

National Service

Conscription into the services continued after the end of the war ensuring continued used of some of the airbases. Redevelopment took place at Feltwell, Langham, Little Snoring and North Pickenham in Norfolk, Horham, Shepherds Grove and Tuddenham in Suffolk, Graveley and Mepal in Cambridgeshire and Woolfox Lodge near Grantham in Lincolnshire.

With the end of National service in 1963, and the re-allocation of the defence budget, the Government decided that even more airfields were surplus to requirements and therefore closed them down. Due to modern technology, aircraft, missiles and defence systems were becoming very much more sophisticated. Fewer bases were required but the ones that remained had to extend their sphere of activities to cope with the new equipment.

Remains of airfields

Remains of a Lincolnshire runway with disused control tower in background.

But where are the ghosts? Men who knew the drama of the scramble or watched the bomb-laden Lancasters and Stirlings roaring down the runway into a beautiful East Anglian sky have memories of the sights and sounds of wartime airfields. But what is left to remind them, or us, of where these stations stood? Dotted here and there, usually unheralded, are some gaunt relics of buildings which once knew busier days. Spotting these remains can be a real work of detection. On the Ordnance Survey maps, 1:50,000, the stations which had concrete runways are clearly marked, and time can be passed most pleasantly by driving or cycling to one of these sites to see what is left. The sites which had no concrete runways, such as Docking and Bircham Newton, are rather harder to spot from the Ordnance Survey maps. However, a reference book, such as ACTION STATIONS by Michael Bowyer, provides enough clues to enable you to discover derelict control towers, Nissen huts, hangars and many other inter-war year buildings.

Having found an airfield, it must be remembered that they are all on private ground and permission must be sought before exploration can begin. There can be a great sense of discovery as one treads the land, looking through idly swinging windows and empty doorways, attempting to reconstruct the geography of the airfield, and imagining it as it once was.

Old buildings and water tower at R.A.F. Sculthorpe

A few odd huts, a water tower, and traceable remnants of runways can excite the enthusiast's imagination as, like a piece of jigsaw puzzle, the features of the airfield can be fitted together to form a complete picture.

Bircham Newton in Norfolk is worthy of a special mention, as here can be seen a number of buildings from the First World War and from inter-war days. The squash courts date back to 1917 and, around midnight on a certain night in March, a ghost of a World War I pilot is reputed to visit there on some eternal quest.

The Construction Industry Training Board has its headquarters at Bircham Newton base now and although huge changes have been made, many of the original buildings are still used.

What else is there left to see?

It has been said that England was a vast aircraft carrier and that, had there been any more aircraft in Eastern England, it would have tipped into the sea under their weight. Certainly the number of aerodromes was vast: 24 in Cambridgeshire, 23 in Essex, 46 in Lincolnshire/South Humberside, 36 in Norfolk and 32 in Suffolk.
There are hundreds of buildings associated with wartime throughout the whole Eastern region, just a few of which are mentioned in the following paragraphs. The map opposite shows most of the sites operated by the R.A..F. and the U.S.A.F. this century.

Astrodome at Langham

Throughout the whole area many of the aerodromes have been taken over by flying and gliding clubs which make use of the old runways, hangars and control towers, as at Swanton Morley in Norfolk. Others are owned by a variety of commercial organisations. For example, the base at Langham now houses a large poultry enterprise and from the roadside an astrodome and a well-renovated control tower can be seen. Other sites are more difficult to find. At Matlaske nothing obvious announces that there was once an airbase, but if you follow the track across the fields, once a runway, the remains of a 'pillbox' can be seen, as well as entrances to underground bomb shelters in the concrete standing. Similarly, at Docking, near Kings Lynn, nothing can be seen from the road but take the Brancaster road out of the village until you come to a fork of the roads, after about a mile, where there is a clump of pine trees. In this clump you will see the remains of old brick huts, said to have been cook houses, entrances to underground bomb shelters, a number of storage buildings and a dilapidated control tower, faintly bearing the painted legend "All pilots report here". The actual aerodrome at Docking was on Sutherland Farm, built on land commandeered in 1938 and not handed back to farming until 1958. It was used as a Coastal Command Station and on one occasion when it was attacked, bombs destroyed a large two-storey farm building and damaged part of the Sutherland Farm house.

Still more of the airfields have been put to exemplary use and now house aviation museums. The most famous one is at Duxford in Cambridgeshire, but others are at Norwich Airport, Bungay in Suffolk and East Kirkby, Lincolnshire. In each case the original buildings are there for you to inspect as well as marvellous collections of aircraft and memorabilia.

Circular 'pillbox' guarding perimeter of Kings Cliffe Airfield.

Spittalgate base in Lincolnshire, just outside Grantham, was vacated by the R.A.F. in 1975 and taken over by the Army. The buildings are still in use and many of them can be seen from the roadside.

Access to operational R.A.F. and U.S.A.F. stations is also possible on occasions such as open days and, of course, the Battle of Britain Flight can be viewed at R.A.F. Coningsby all year round.

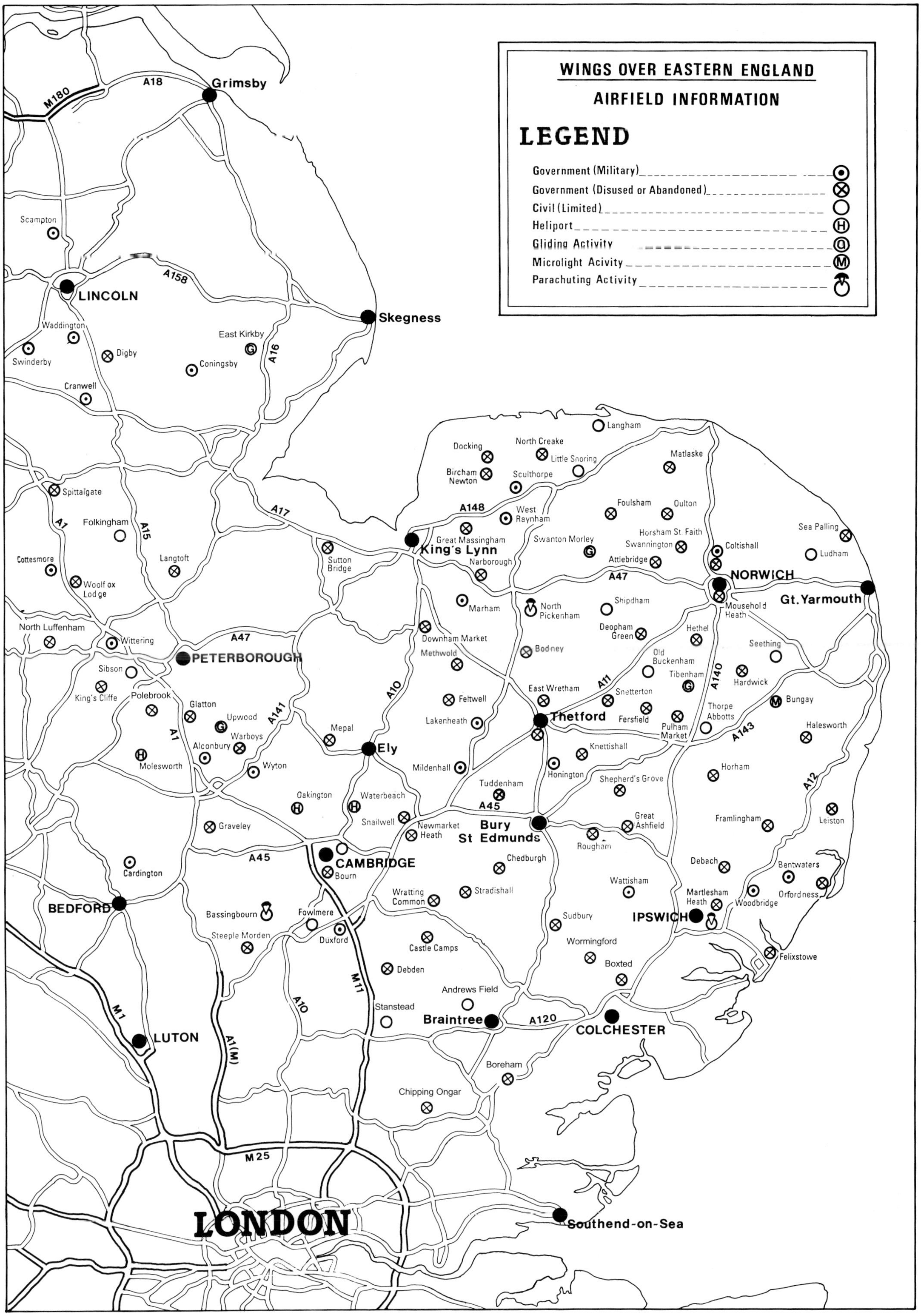
WINGS OVER EASTERN ENGLAND
AIRFIELD INFORMATION
LEGEND
Government (Military)
Government (Disused or Abandoned)
Civil (Limited)
Heliport
Gliding Activity
Microlight Acivity
Parachuting Activity
Grimsby
M180
A18
Scampton
LINCOLN
A158
Skegness
Waddington
Swinderby
Digby
East Kirkby
Coningsby
A16
Cranwell
Spittalgate
A1
Folkingham
A15
Cottesmore
Woolf ox Lodge
Langtoft
A17
Sutton Bridge
King's Lynn
North Luffenham
Wittering
A47
PETERBOROUGH
Sibson
King's Cliffe
Polebrook
Glatton
Upwood
Warboys
A141
Alconbury
Molesworth
Wyton
Mepal
Ely
A10
Oakington
Waterbeach
Snailwell
Graveley
A45
CAMBRIDGE
Bourn
Cardington
BEDFORD
Bassingbourn
Fowlmere
Duxford
Steeple Morden
M11
M1
LUTON
A1(M)
Stanstead
Langham
Docking
North Creake
Little Snoring
Bircham Newton
Sculthorpe
Matlaske
A148
West Raynham
Great Massingham
Narborough
Foulsham
Oulton
Horsham St. Faith
Swannington
Swanton Morley
Attlebridge
Coltishall
Sea Palling
Ludham
NORWICH
Gt. Yarmouth
Mousehold Heath
Marham
North Pickenham
Shipdham
Deopham Green
Downham Market
Methwold
Bodney
Hethel
Old Buckenham
Tibenham
Seething
Hardwick
A140
Feltwell
East Wretham
A11
Snetterton
Bungay
Lakenheath
Thetford
Fersfield
Pulham Market
Thorpe Abbotts
A143
Halesworth
Knettishall
Mildenhall
Honington
Tuddenham
Shepherd's Grove
Horham
A12
Great Ashfield
Framlingham
Leiston
Newmarket Heath
Bury St Edmunds
Rougham
Chedburgh
Debach
Bentwaters
Wattisham
Martlesham Heath
Woodbridge
Orfordness
Wratting Common
Stradishall
Sudbury
IPSWICH
Castle Camps
Wormingford
Felixstowe
Debden
Boxted
Andrews Field
Braintree
A120
COLCHESTER
Boreham
Chipping Ongar
M25
LONDON
Southend-on-Sea

And the Story Goes On

Some airfields continued in use until the present day and operational flying can still be seen at some of them. The U.S.A.F. have continued to maintain Alconbury, Mildenhall and Lakenheath. These bases are still very much alive, even though their operations have changed vastly since 1945, but Woodbridge and Bentwaters are due for closure in 1993. Similar changes have taken place at the R.A. F. stations, many of which are fully operational, although not all are used as flying bases.

Aerial view of Mildenhall

There have been great changes in the aeronautical world since the war. Air Sea Rescue, various emergencies, wars and general alert situations have all affected the direction which the R.A.F. has taken, but the greatest impact has been made in the areas of aircraft and missile design.

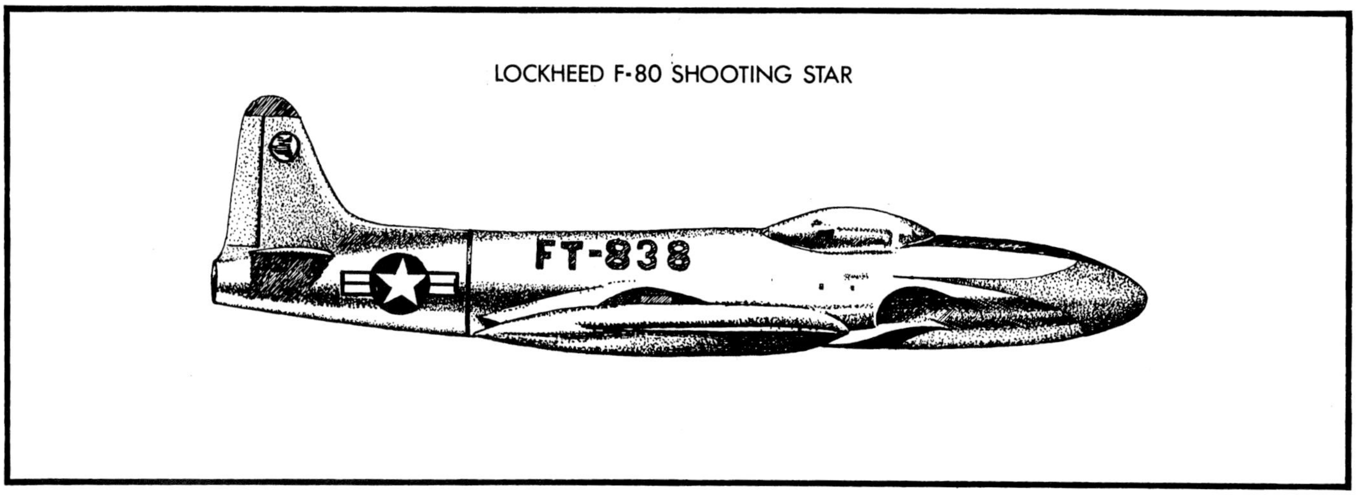

Enter the Jets

At the end of the war the familiar Mustangs, Mosquitos, Spitfires and Hornets were still flying from Coltishall, Duxford and Horsham St. Faith, but already the jet engine, developed in 1941, was in service. The Gloster Meteor, introduced in 1944 as the first R.A.F. jet fighter, was the only Allied jet in action. The first Mark I's were delivered to 616 Squadron, then flying from Debden in Essex, in July 1944. The Americans also were involved in research and development work on the jet engine in the United States, but introduction of new craft on their Eastern airfields was slow. Britain, with the Meteor and Vampire fighters, plus the English Electric Canberra bomber, was well ahead. However, once the war in Japan ceased, the American aeronautical industry developed rapidly, producing the Thunderjet and Shooting Star among others.

Missiles versus Bombers

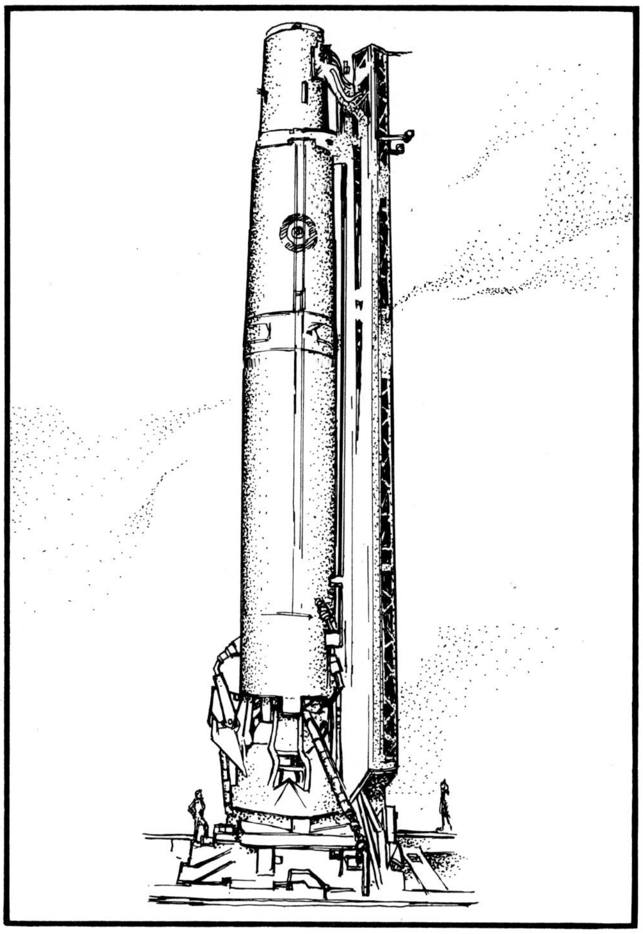

The Thor Intermediate Range Ballistic Missile

Perhaps as a result of the German V2 rocket raids, during the 1950's Western and Soviet powers began to develop unmanned rocket propelled weapons. Inter-Continental Ballistic Missiles capable of carrying large warheads could hit targets without warning, and were unstoppable. Smaller missiles, air-to-air, ground-to-ground and even air-to-ground, which were rocket propelled and faster than then current aircraft, were developed to destroy them. The bomber seemed redundant. Many airfields were secretly converted to rocket-launching sites for ICBM's, shorter range 'strategic' missiles and anti-aircraft defence missiles. Of the latter it was thought that if a battery of 12 were fired at once, any aircraft within a square mile would be caught in a suction vortex and plummet to earth!

In the Eastern Counties, Thor missiles were based at a number of stations including Coleby Grange and Woolfox Lodge in Lincolnshire, Warboys in Cambridgeshire and Little Snoring in Norfolk. However, new technological developments showed that a very fast manned jet aircraft, flying outside radar detection capability, could 'take out' an I.C.B.M. sited above ground in the time it was being prepared for firing. Most I.C.B.M.'s then went into underground bunkers and less easily located submarines.

The new jet-engined aircraft required superior runways and more sophisticated support systems so many famous bases were modernised. Afterwards, sightings of the British Meteor, Vampire, Javelin, Venom and Hunter fighters, Canberra, Valiant, Victor and Vulcan bombers, and the Comet airliner, the first jet-propelled passenger aircraft, became common-place. Occasionally the sound of the sonic 'boom' would be heard as an aircraft dived from great height to pass through the speed of the 'sound barrier'. Soon afterwards came the exciting Lightning fighter, the first squadron service aircraft capable of exceeding the speed of sound in level flight, and the Buccaneer, a very fast, very low-level strike aircraft.

B.A.C. Lightnings taking off at R.A.F. Coltishall

The V Bomber Force

A 1970's Vulcan V Bomber

The V Bombers were a tremendously exciting development, for here was the answer to the missile threat in the shape of fast, big aircraft able to discharge weapons capable of terrific destruction. The V Bomber force was made up by Valiants stationed at R.A.F. Marham, Wittering and Wyton and Victors at Honington and Vulcans at Waddington. Tremendous faith was placed in these high flying 'planes and thus so much greater was the dismay when it was found that the Valiant was subject to fatigue problems when switched to low-flying. Vulcans were used in the 1982 war with Argentina over the Falkland Islands and one was still based at R.A.F. Waddington in the early 1990's.

And on the Fringe

Martlesham and Watton were used as experimental and development stations, Feltwell assumed a training role, and the Coltishall satellite radar station at Neatishead provided a valuable early warning system.

Thus the 1950s and 1960s were times of streamlining development and in the few stations left in Eastern England there grew a far greater striking force than the whole of the area had possessed during the Second World War.

The Americans

The development of the U.S.A.A.F. bases evolved in a very similar way to the R.A.F. stations. At Alconbury the runways were extended and in the fifties the station became the home of great bombers such as the B-45 Tornado, troop carriers such as the C-47 Skytrain and the amphibious SA-16 Albatross. At Bentwaters great excitement was aroused when the first F-86A Sabres arrived but before the end of the 1950's its role was to change twice. It became the home of the 81st Fighter Interceptor Group in 1951 and was officially assigned to Headquarters 3rd Air Force. The great Thunderstreak bombers arrived in 1954, followed by the F-101 Voodoo's in 1958. Lakenheath was the base for the 2nd Bombardment Group flying, among others, the RB-36 Convair heavy bombers. In 1954 the station changed its role when the B-47 Stratojet tankers arrived. Sculthorpe enjoyed various roles, including acting as a base for reconnaissance planes and bombers and the mighty force of seventy- five B-45 bombers was later stationed there.

Sea King Helicopter on route to R.A.F. Coltishall

Air Sea Rescue

One of the four flights of the Search and Rescue Service (previously designated the Air Sea Rescue) in Great Britain is based at Coltishall in the form of 202 Squadron. Flying Sea King Mark 3 helicopters, which alternate with 22 Squadron flying Wessex helicopters, their task is to rescue British and Allied aircrew, but requests from the police and coastguards add to their duties. There is a crew permanently on standby and they can be airborne within fifteen minutes of a call.

During the years the S.A.R. service has carried out many notable rescues. On the 27th April, 1963, Flight Lieutenant Burns, flying a B.A.C. Lightning from Coltishall over the Cromer area on a training flight, was in great danger when, at a height of 10,000 feet (3,000 metres) the plane caught fire. Leaving little time for action at such a height and speed, Flt. Lt. Burns merely radioed his distress and position before parachuting safely into a field near Cromer. Within twenty minutes he was back at his base, for his call had brought a Coltishall Whirlwind to his aid.

On the 14th June of the same year another Whirlwind from Coltishall accomplished a remarkable rescue mission when it searched for the Lowestoft trawler Trinidad which was in a bank of thick fog about twenty miles (12.5 km) off Cromer. A member of the crew had suffered a massive drug overdose and had to be hospitalised to save his life. In spite of the fog and low cloud, the trawler was found and the crewman was ferried to Cromer hospital just in time.

Captain James Evans and First Lieutenant George Kuprian of the U.S.A.A.F. were flying a F4D Phantom on a training flight over the North Sea just off Great Yarmouth on 22nd November, 1975. Suddenly their aircraft engine failed and they had to eject and parachute down to the eight foot (2.5 metres) waves beneath. Within thirty minutes of their landing in the water they were spotted by a Coltishall Whirlwind and carried safely back to Lakenheath.

Thirty miles north east of Cromer on the afternoon of January 10, 1991, a rig standby ship, the St Martin, was taking a pounding from waves up to twenty feet high. When it became obvious that she was going under the crew put out a distress call, and prepared to board the liferaft. Within 30 minutes of the distress call going out the vessel had disappeared out of sight, under the raging sea, but also within that thirty minutes all eight crew members had been winched to safety and were on their way, to the James Paget Hospital in Gorleston. Another job well done.

View from the rescue helicopter as they prepared to pluck the seamen from the 'St Martin' in January 1991.

The story of 202 Squadron goes on and it is appropriate that their motto should be "Always Alert".

Hawker Harrier

When the Hawker Harrier Jump Jet entered service with the R.A.F. in April 1969, it was the worlds first operational vertical take-off aircraft. It combined the capabilities of a helicopter with the speed of a fighter and can be operated from a clearing the size of a tennis court. This factor enables the Harrier to be dispersed and operated from any suitable field or woodland should its airfield be attacked. Also flown by the Royal Navy as Sea Harriers, this revolutionary aircraft has rendered heavy aircraft carriers obsolete and was the subject of interest all over the world. The Harrier is now flown by the Spanish air force and is being further developed in the United States where it is manufactured under licence.

Harrier GR Mk 3 landing at Wittering

Through the Seventies and into the Eighties

These years saw continued commitment to aircraft design, more streamlining of airfields, the use of very expensive machines, high cost maintenance, well-trained crews and first class buildings and equipment.

Each R.A.F. base had its special role: Wittering was known for its Harriers, Marham for its Tornados and the three squadrons forming the air element of the United Kingdom Mobile Force were based at Coltishall. Their Jaguars could be heard screaming overhead as they took part in training missions, and occasionally a helicopter could be seen taking off for a Search and Rescue mission. Honington became a high security base in the early 1970's, the home of the TV guided Martel missiles.

The Americans continued to maintain a balanced force in East Anglia to honour their N.A.T.O. commitments, operating from eight main bases.

Phantoms and TR-1 photo-reconnaissance 'planes were based at Alconbury as was the 527 Tactical Fighter Training Aggressor Squadron from 1976 until its transfer to Bentwaters in 1988. At this time Alconbury received the Thunderbolt II's that had been based at

Sepecat Jaguar GR Mk 1

Bentwaters and supported by the 48th Tactical Fighter Wing's F111's at Lakenheath. The huge complex at Mildenhall housed tankers, reconnaissance aircraft and the naval air facility but Sculthorpe was gradually run down until its closure in 1990. The exciting 67th Aerospace Rescue and Recovery Squadron, flying the Jolly Green Giant helicopters, was active at Woodbridge, and at Molesworth there was action of a different sort. For years it was a storage depot but in 1985 the R.A.F. prepared Molesworth to become a centre for the ground launched Cruise nuclear missiles. The arrival of the missiles and the handing back of control to the U.S. the following year caused a storm of protest which did not truly abate until their withdrawal in 1988/9 after the Americans and Russians agreed to limit intermediate-range missiles.

Technology on the March

Throughout these peaceful decades, engineers and scientists worked away at incredibly interesting projects and every aspect of aeronautics was affected. New types of ejector seats were provided for the aircrew which had built-in safety features and, indeed the cockpit of modern aircraft was not even remotely comparable with their 1940's counterparts.

Type 9B Martin Baker Jaguar Ejector Seat

Mid-air refuelling became possible, thus ending the necessity for journeys to distant locations to be done in short hops, to facilitate refuelling. A number of 'planes, including the Valiant, Hercules, VC10 and Boeing 707 can be used as flying 'tankers', feeding fuel to 'families' of the smaller fighters and bombers. The R.A.F. uses hoses, the 'probe and drogue' technique and the U.S.A.F. favour the 'boom and slipway' system. Keen observers will have seen the Boeing KC-135 Stratotankers at Mildenhall. Carrying some 26,000 gallons of fuel, they position themselves in pre-arranged areas so that aircraft on missions may top-up their tanks. This 'mother and chicks' arrangement proved invaluable on the flights to the Falkland Islands and became a familiar sight on our television screens during the Gulf War.

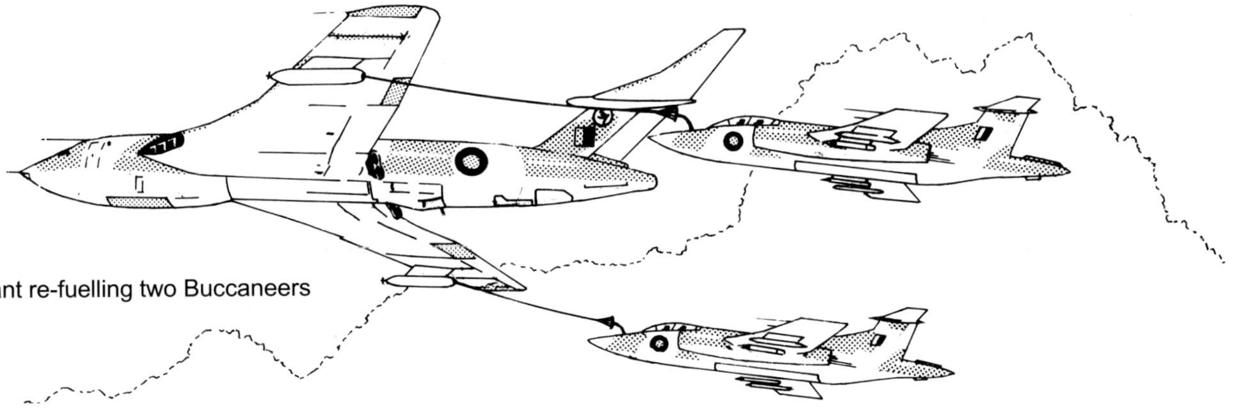

Valiant re-fuelling two Buccaneers

High Tech Espionage and Electronic Warfare

A radar station in the sky is one way of describing the British Aerospace Nimrod. This is an airborne early warning aircraft with a huge bulbous nose and similarly extended tail fuselage and could be seen flying from Waddington and Wyton. Unfortunately the radar specification could not be attained by the manufacturers and orders for the Nimrod, based on the Comet airliner, were cancelled. There are some still flying, but in the role of marine reconnaissance/anti-submarine aircraft, and without their bulbous appendages.

B.Ae. Nimrod at Alconbury in 1990

The Boeing E-3A Sentry airborne warning and control (AWAC) aircraft, with its startling huge 'mushroom' or 'umbrella' fitting standing up on top, can be seen operating from the U.S.A.F. base at Mildenhall and R.A.F. Waddington. Being able to 'see' electronically all land and air movements within a large area, this aircraft is used to control friendly aircraft to position them against threatening air strikes, land missile strikes or even hostile troop movements.

The Blackbird, or Lockheed SR-71, one of the most spectacular aircraft ever seen, was operated from Mildenhall and Alconbury but withdrawn from service in 1990. It was a strategic reconnaissance aircraft and reputedly the fasted true aircraft (as opposed to rocket powered experimental aircraft), flying more than three times the speed of sound and at edge-of-space altitudes. It was capable of photographing territory with amazing detail and clarity but was recently superceded by spy satellites. The Blackbird was uniquely beautiful, yet it also had a sinister appearance, and even now it is surrounded by secrecy.

Blackbird at Mildenhall – since superceded by satellites.

The Lockheed TR-1 tactical reconnaissance aircraft can be seen flying from Alconbury. Its lengthy slender body with tapered long narrow wings make it easily identifiable and it appears to fly quite slowly. Designed to collect visual and electronic information from an altitude of 17 miles this aircraft supercedes the U2 version, one of which was shot down whilst on a mission over Russia in 1960 when the pilot, Gary Powers, parachuted down and was detained by the Russian authorities.

S6 Respirator currently issued to all R.A.F. personnel for use in case of nuclear, chemical or biological attack.

The Tornado

The Tornado Multi-Role Combat Aircraft entered R.A.F. service in the 1980's and heralded an entirely new approach to warfare. It was by far the most advanced aircraft flying in Europe and its development was a joint venture between Britain, Germany and Italy. Designed to take the place of Vulcans, Canberras and Phantoms, the plan was to base Tornados at some of the smaller, less sophisticated stations including Cottesmore and Marham.

Since its introduction to active service this fighter bomber has played many high profile roles and proved its worth over and over again, especially recently as many of them were deployed in the Gulf.

The Tornado probably is the aircraft that the public knows most about because of the media coverage of the Tornados and their crews at the beginning of 1991 during the battle known as 'Desert Storm'. The period of preparation and troop build-up in Saudi Arabia during the last third of 1990 was known as 'Desert Shield' and during this time Tornados from a number of different countries, including Saudi Arabia and Italy, were preparing for conflict. In the case of the Tornados coming from Eastern England, this also meant a change of appearance. They were repainted in desert camouflage colours and some had sharks teeth painted near their noses.

Tornado Multi-Role combat aircraft

Tornado bases in Eastern England include Cottesmore, Coningsby, Honington and Marham and it is flown by air forces throughout the world. It's capabilities are almost legendary and its cost phenomenal – each plane costs £20-million. The electronic equipment on board makes it possible to pin-point targets for perfect attack accuracy, and each mission is pre-recorded into a cassette and inserted into the navigation system. They have air re-fuelling probes which allow them to fly deep into enemy territory and, because of their terrain following radar, can fly at night, at 500mph just 50 feet from the ground. In ideal circumstances they fly at more than 1,500mph. Its swing-wings allow the pilots greater manoeuvrability which gives them a better chance to escape from dangerous situations.

The aircrew is very well protected in their computerised cockpit which has electronic surveillance measures to spot enemy radar and missiles. The GR1 version, which was used in the Gulf, was equipped with the JP233 anti-runway bomb which, in 1991, cost more than £1-million each. They are able to release flares and chaff to confuse enemy radar and missiles and targets can be spotted by their laser range finders. The Tornado is a very impressive machine indeed, which the R.A.F. will continue to use as we approach the 21st Century.

What does the future hold? On order from B.Ae. is the E.F.A., or European Fighter Aircraft, which is due to come into service in 1995 but apart from that nothing else is public knowledge.

Chapter 6. ACTION STATIONS AGAIN

At the beginning of the 1980's Europe was a very peaceful place although the same could not be said about the rest of the world. There was always the threat of a larger conflict in the Middle East where Saddam Hussein of Iraq was already at war with Iran.

In Eastern England, however, the peace of the skies was only broken by the regular whining of the A10's and the screaming of the F111's, Tornados, Jaguars, Harriers and Phantoms as they practised low level flying over our flatlands, and civilian aircraft moving towards their destinations.

Phantoms in low flying formation

The R.A.F. story continued amidst the brave traditions of the service and the constant thrill of flight. No-one, back in 1980, could have foretold with certainty that within the next 12 years planes would leave the Eastern skies three times in anger.

Watching aircraft taking off and landing has always been a fascinating pastime. See the lumbering Galaxy transporters at Mildenhall and compare them with the liquid speed of the Jaguars at Coltishall. Open Days and Air Displays are regularly held at a number of places throughout the region and are always well advertised through local media.

Benevolent Associations

Most of the funds raised by the R.A.F. at their open events are donated to the R.A.F.A. which spends the money most carefully. With branches in most towns and cities of Eastern England, the R.A.F.A. is a charitable institution very like its sister organisation the British Legion, whose objective is to assist personnel and their families after death or injury in the service. Those injured may be given advice about obtaining an adequate pension, or may be granted assistance for any retraining which may be necessary in order to prepare for a suitable civilian occupation. The clubs that they run are very good social centres.

As an official observer, Group Captain Leonard Cheshire watched the bomb drop on Hiroshima and felt such remorse at the outcome that he and his wife decided to set up establishments for those displaced by war. Barnes Wallis designed the bouncing bomb for use as dam busters but could not foresee the losses incurred by 617 Squadron who flew the missions. He was shocked by the outcome, and donated all of his earnings from the development of the bomb to the widows and orphans of the pilots concerned.

Two war-time airmen and their Spitfire

During the last decade special counselling services have been set up for the personnel and their families who have been through the trauma of active service.

In these and similar ways the comradeship of the R.A.F., and the responsibility they show to each other, is continued

The Falklands War

In April 1982 Argentinian forces, who had long felt that the territory known to them as the Malvinas belonged to Argentina, seized the Falkland Islands. Britain had a war on her hands and once more the sound of angry aeroplane noises was heard along the flightpaths of Eastern England as the R.A.F. went on standby.

This was essentially a Naval war, using Sea Harriers, but the R.A.F. was called upon to supply additional support.

Three Vulcan bombers flew non-stop from Waddington to their new base on Ascension Island and were used on the 'Black Buck' runs designed to destroy the runway at the Argentine-occupied airfield at Port Stanley. For these raids the Vulcans had to be refuelled eight times on each round trip. One of these bombers can still be seen today on the western edge of R.A.F. Waddinton's airfield.

Handley Page Victor from R.A.F. Marham, one of those used for refuelling on the way to the Falkland Islands.

1 (Fighter) Squadron from R.A.F. Wittering, flying Harrier GR3's, headed towards the South Atlantic too. The Navy's Sea Harriers were fairly stretched covering the Task Force, therefore extra air power was required in reconnaissance and low level ground attack roles. Even in Antarctic gales, these Harriers performed their tasks brilliantly: the expense of the trials, training and exercises was justified.

Many other 'planes from Eastern England were involved, including a number of Victors from Marham which were used for mid-air refuelling. Phantoms from Coningsby concentrated on air defence of the Ascension Islands and post-war they were moved to Port Stanley to protect the Falklands – after the runway had been extended by 2000 feet to accommodate them! It is said that Nimrods and Canberras from Wyton were active during the conflict too. After the Argentinian surrender, Sea Kings from Coltishall were taken out there to perform Search and Rescue missions.

With the Falklands War behind them the R.A.F. settled down once more to everyday life. Low flying exercises over the Wash, coastal patrols, trials, rescue missions, training, ferrying around troops, equipment and VIP's – and flying displays.

Hawker Siddeley Harrier vertical take-off fighter based at R.A.F. Wittering.

The Red Arrows

The Red Arrows flying the Tango Roll, the most demanding manoeuvre in their repertoire because it is extremely difficult to maintain five aircraft line abreast all the way round a barrel roll. Photograph: MoD copyright.

For public relations, publicity and building up the prestige of the R.A.F., the aerobatic displays by the Red Arrows cannot be beaten. They are recognised and admired all over the world, with their skill and confidence never in doubt. Aerobatics are actually just part of a pilots training but in the case of the Red Arrows pilots, based at R.A.F. Scampton, near Lincoln, they go those few steps further. The Squadron's peacetime role is to demonstrate the qualities and skills of airmen but, if needed, they would be absorbed into operational squadrons. Their 'planes are BAe Hawk T Mk 1's, which are single-engined two-seater ground attack/trainer aircraft, and can be adapted to carry 30mm cannons and Sidewinder missiles.

There are nine display pilots in the Squadron and between them some 24,000 flying hours have been amassed. Most have served ten years in the R.A.F. and their Red Arrows tours will last for three years. Each winter three new pilots join them, thus combining an injection of 'new blood' and the maintenance of an experienced foundation for the team. The Red Arrows back-up team is quite extensive and for any one show up to fifty personnel could be involved, requiring a Hercules to transport them and everything that they need.

Throughout the Spring, Summer and Autumn thousands of people are spellbound by their weaving, rolling and wheeling, all confined to an area that enables the public to keep them in sight at all times. The sheer perfection of the formations held as they go through their amazing routine is a credit to the pilots and it is comforting to know that, after their three year tour of duty, some of them will be instructing the next generation of R.A.F. pilots. In 1989 they celebrated their 25th display season and each year their repertoire grows – watch the press for details of Red Arrows displays and do yourself a favour: go and watch.

Private Airfields

Many of the old war-time fields still echo the sound of aeroplane engines but now the aircraft are vastly different. They are generally the single-engined trainers and private planes which are flown by wealthy individuals, private flying clubs or commercial concerns. A crop-spraying company is based at Foulsham in Norfolk, a flying school at Holbeach St Johns in Lincolnshire, a parachute club at Sibson in Cambridgeshire, short airtours can be enjoyed by holiday-makers at Skegness and Great Yarmouth and the Air Training Corps Gliding School use Swanton Morley. Hethel Airfield, near Wymondham in Norfolk, was once a U.S.A.A.F. base operating Liberators but is now mainly owned by Lotus Cars.

Small private aircraft

A Request from the President

In the early summer of 1986 the British Prime Minister received a request for assistance from the President of the United States. President Ghaddafi of Libya was reportedly backing international terrorists who had been directly responsible for the death of American citizens and retaliation was planned. Because of the distances involved, it would have been difficult for the American Air Force to complete the raid from home territory to North Africa and they wanted to use aircraft from a European base. The Prime Minister gave her permission for U.S.A.F. F111's based at Lakenheath to be deployed and a number of aircrews took part.

General dynamics F111 based at Lakenheath

The East Anglian Airport

New Terminal at Stanstead Airport

The Airport at Stanstead in Essex has been operational for many years but is undergoing massive development which will eventually enable it to handle 15,000,000 passengers each year. The new terminal, which opened in 1991, forms just part of the £400-million investment plan and allows holidaymakers and other air travellers to enjoy the most up-to-date facilities. A number of airlines already use Stanstead, which has the space to be twice the size of Gatwick airport, and many types of aeroplanes can be seen landing and taking off. Road and rail links to Stanstead are improving all the time and this provides benefits for countless people.

War in the Gulf

On the 2nd August 1990 the Iraqi armed forces, under the command of their President, Saddam Hussein, invaded Kuwait and the world was not slow to voice its disapproval. The United Nations imposed a trade embargo, backed up by the threat of military action, and by 8th August the first American troops had arrived in Saudi Arabia. The same day Iraq declared that it was annexing Kuwait. Three days later the first British aircraft left for the Gulf. Alongside heavy diplomatic activity, the Allied troops were massing in the Gulf and by Christmas they numbered about half a million. Many R.A.F. planes went out there, including AWACS reconnaissance aircraft, refuelling tankers and Coltishall's Jaguars. Members of the famous 'Dam Busters' 617 Squadron from Marham went with their Tornados – and a new nickname: 'Saddam Busters'. Iraq defied the U.N. deadline of 15th January, refusing to leave Kuwait, consequently two days later the battle known as 'Desert Storm' started with an Air War.

Airman of the 90's – of the Rapier Squadron based at Honiton.

The Allies wanted this war over with quickly and endeavoured to 'take out' certain strategic targets in Baghdad, hoping to cut communications and damage the city's infrastructure. 'Smart bombs' were used, hitting targets with pin-point accuracy and leaving adjacent buildings intact.

The Jaguar and Tornado aircrews had exceedingly difficult and demanding missions to fly, involving a lot of extremely low flying. The Tornados of 617 Squadron were deployed to put the Iraqi airfields out of action, screaming in at 600 m.p.h. less than 100 feet above the ground, to drop their JP233 runway bombs. 52 – 8

Even though the technology is incomparable, the emotions experienced during a mission by the modern airmen will be identical to those felt by the 1940's Few: fear, apprehension, thrill of flight, total concentration, and relief. The Spitfire and Hurricane pilots, however, may have only had 20 hours flying practice, whereas the 1990's airmen are extremely well trained and very experienced.

Jaguar from R.A.F. Coltishall, deployed in the Gulf War.

Fleets of U.S.A.F. A10 Thunderbolts from Alconbury and Bentwaters were deployed in the Gulf, accompanied by more than 3000 support staff. They are often called 'Tankbusters', probably are as close as can be to a flying tank, and have no radar assistance. Their main

A Fairchild A10 Thunderbolt antitank aircraft based at Bentwaters. Commonly known as Tankbusters, they were widely deployed in the Gulf War.

roles were to drop cluster bombs on Iraqi tanks, hunt out and destroy Scud missile launchers, and attack infantry concentrations. During a search of the desert for missing aircrew, it was a Thunderbolt pilot who spotted a U.S.A.F. airman and kept guard over him until the rescue helicopter arrived. They are amazing aircraft, built to withstand direct hits from ground missiles, with an excellent safety record. The pilot sits in a cockpit, which has been likened to a bathtub, protected by titanium, and if it is necessary for him to eject, then the whole cockpit blows out with him. 143 – 10

Over 110,000 individual sorties were flown by the Allies, 42 Allied aircraft were lost in action, billions of pounds spent and too many lives lost, before Iraq surrendered on March 3rd, 1991.

So, the War in the Gulf is over for now, but it was not a satisfactory conclusion. Saddam Hussein is still refusing to comply with the agreed terms of the ceasefire and there is always the possibility that the aeroplanes from Coltishall, Marham and Alconbury will have to return.

Since the end of the Cold War and the decline of communism, our enemies are not so easy to define and United Kingdom defence policy changes to suit the international climate. With this in mind, 1 Squadron and their Harriers, currently based at R.A.F. Wittering, will become part of a N.A.T.O. Rapid Reaction Force, a multi-national force which will be used to respond to international incidents. Whatever changes the future may bring, Eastern England will always be known for its importance in the history of flight.

The 1991 Passing Our Parade at R.A.F. Cranwell: Photograph used by kind permission of the A.O.C. and Commandant, Royal Air Force College, Cranwell.